The Island by Lord L ̣

or, CHRISTIAN AND HIS COMRADES.

George Gordon Byron, 6th Baron Byron, but more commonly known as just Byron was a leading English poet in the Romantic Movement along with Keats and Shelley.

Byron was born on January 22nd, 1788. He was a great traveller across Europe, spending many years in Italy and much time in Greece. With his aristocratic indulgences, flamboyant style along with his debts, and a string of lovers he was the constant talk of society.

In 1823 he joined the Greeks in their war of Independence against the Ottoman Empire, both helping to fund and advise on the war's conduct.

It was an extraordinary adventure, even by his own standards. But, for us, it is his poetry for which he is mainly remembered even though it is difficult to see where he had time to write his works of immense beauty. But write them he did.

He died on April 19th 1824 after having contracted a cold which, on the advice of his doctors, was treated with blood-letting. This cause complications and a violent fever set in. Byron died like his fellow romantics, tragically young and on some foreign field.

Index of Contents
Introduction to the Island
Advertisement
Canto the first
Canto the Second
Canto the Third
Canto the Fourth
Lord Byron - A Short Biography
Lord Byron - A Concise Bibliography

INTRODUCTION TO THE ISLAND

The first canto of The Island was finished January 10, 1823. We know that Byron was still at work on "the poeshie," January 25 (Letters, 1901, vi. 164), and may reasonably conjecture that a somewhat illegible date affixed to the fourth canto, stands for February 14, 1823. The MS. had been received in London before April 9 (ibid., p. 192); and on June 26, 1823, The Island; or, The Adventures of Christian and his Comrades, was published by John Hunt.

Byron's "Advertisement," or note, prefixed to The Island contains all that need be said with regard to the "sources" of the poem.

Two separate works were consulted: (1) A Narrative of the Mutiny on board His Majesty's Ship Bounty, and the subsequent Voyage of ... the Ship's Boat from Tafoa, one of the Friendly Islands, to Timor, a Dutch Settlement in the East Indies, written by Lieutenant William Bligh, 1790; and (2) An

Account of the Natives of the Tonga Islands, Compiled and Arranged from the Extensive Communications of Mr. William Mariner, by John Martin, M.D., 1817.

According to George Clinton (Life and Writings of Lord Byron, 1824, p. 656), Byron was profoundly impressed by Mariner's report of the scenery and folklore of the Friendly Islands, was "never tired of talking of it to his friends," and, in order to turn this poetic material to account, finally bethought him that Bligh's Narrative of the mutiny of the Bounty would serve as a framework or structure "for an embroidery of rare device"—the figures and foliage of a tropical pattern. That, at least, is the substance of Clinton's analysis of the "sources" of The Island, and whether he spoke, or only feigned to speak, with authority, his criticism is sound and to the point. The story of the mutiny of the Bounty, which is faithfully related in the first canto, is not, as the second title implies, a prelude to the "Adventures of Christian and his Comrades," but to a description of "The Island," an Ogygia of the South Seas.

It must be borne in mind that Byron's acquaintance with the details of the mutiny of the Bounty was derived exclusively from Bligh's Narrative; that he does not seem to have studied the minutes of the court-martial on Peter Heywood and the other prisoners (September, 1792), or to have possessed the information that in 1809, and, again, in 1815, the Admiralty received authentic information with regard to the final settlement of Christian and his comrades on Pitcairn Island. Articles, however, had appeared in the Quarterly Review, February, 1810, vol. iii. pp. 23, 24, and July, 1815, vol. xiii. pp. 376-378, which contained an extract from the log-book of Captain Mayhew Folger, of the American ship Topaz, dated September 29, 1808, and letters from Folger (March 1, 1813), and Sir Thomas Staines, October 18, 1814, which solved the mystery. Moreover, the article of February, 1810, is quoted in the notes (pp. 313-318) affixed to Miss Mitford's Christina, the Maid of the South Seas, 1811, a poem founded on Bligh's Narrative, of which neither Byron or his reviewers seem to have heard.

But whatever may have been his opportunities of ascertaining the facts of the case, it is certain (see his note to Canto IV. section vi. line 122) that he did not know what became of Christian, and that whereas in the first canto he follows the text of Bligh's Narrative, in the three last cantos he draws upon his imagination, turning Tahiti into Toobonai (Tubuai), and transporting Toobonai from one archipelago to another—from the Society to the Friendly Islands.

Another and still more surprising feature of The Island is that Byron accepts, without qualification or reserve, the guilt of the mutineers and the innocence and worth of Lieutenant Bligh. It is true that by inheritance he was imbued with the traditions of the service, and from personal experience understood the necessity of discipline on board ship; but it may be taken for granted that if he had known that the sympathy, if not the esteem, of the public had been transferred from Bligh to Christian, that in the opinion of grave and competent writers, the guilt of mutiny on the high seas had been almost condoned by the violence and brutality of the commanding officer, he would have sided with the oppressed rather than the oppressor. As it is, he takes Bligh at his own valuation, and carefully abstains from "eulogizing mutiny." (Letter to L. Hunt, January 25, 1823.)

The story of the "mutiny of the Bounty" happened in this wise. In 1787 it occurred to certain West India planters and merchants, resident in London, that it would benefit the natives, and perhaps themselves, if the bread-fruit tree, which flourished in Tahiti (the Otaheite of Captain Cook and Sir Joseph Banks, see Poetical Works, 1899, ii. 7, note 2) and other islands of the South Seas, could be acclimatized in the West Indies. A petition was addressed to the king, with the result that a vessel, with a burden of 215 tons, which Banks christened the Bounty, sailed from Spithead December 23, 1787. Lieutenant William Bligh, who had sailed with Cook in the Resolution, acted as commanding officer, and under him were five midshipmen, a master, two master's mates, etc.—forty-four persons all told. The Bounty arrived at Tahiti October 26, 1788, and there for six delightful months the ship's company tarried, "fleeting the time carelessly, as in the elder world." But "Scripture saith an ending to all fine things must be," and on April 4, 1789, the Bounty, with a cargo of over a thousand bread-fruit trees, planted in pots, tubs, and boxes (see for plate of the pots, etc., A Voyage, etc., 1792, p. 1), sailed away westward for the Cape of Good Hope, and the West Indies. All went well at first, but "just before sun-rising" on Tuesday, April 28, 1789, "the north-westernmost of the Friendly Islands, called Tofoa, bearing north-east," Fletcher Christian, who was mate of the watch, assisted by Charles Churchill, master-at-arms, Alexander Smith (the John Adams of Pitcairn Island), and Thomas Burkitt, able seamen, seized the captain, tied his hands behind his back, hauled him out of his berth, and forced him on deck. The boatswain, William Cole, was ordered to hoist out the ship's launch, which measured twenty-three feet from stem to stern, and into this open boat Bligh, together with eighteen of the crew, who were or were supposed to be on his side, were thrust, on pain of instant death. When they were in the boat they were "veered round with a rope, and finally cast adrift." Bligh and his eighteen innocent companions sailed westward, and, after a voyage of "twelve hundred leagues," during which they were preserved from death and destruction by the wise ordering and patient heroism of the commander, safely anchored in Kœpang Bay, on the north-west coast of the Isle of Timor, June 14, 1789. (See Bligh's Narrative, etc., 1790, pp. 11-88; and The Island, Canto I. section ix. lines 169-201.)

The Bounty, with the remainder of the crew, twenty-five in number, "the most able of the ship's company," sailed eastward, first to Toobooai, or Tubuai, an island to the south of the Society Islands, thence to Tahiti (June 6), back to Tubuai (June 26), and yet again, to Tahiti (September 20), where sixteen of the mutineers, including the midshipman George Stewart (the "Torquil" of The Island), were put on shore. Finally, September 21, 1789, Fletcher Christian, with the Bounty and eight of her crew, six Tahitian men, and twelve women, sailed away still further east to unknown shores, and, so it was believed, disappeared for good and all. Long afterwards it was known that they had landed on Pitcairn Island, broken up the Bounty, and founded a permanent settlement.

When Bligh returned to England (March 14, 1790), and acquainted the Government "with the atrocious act of piracy and mutiny" which had been committed on the high seas, the Pandora frigate, with Captain Edwards, was despatched to apprehend the mutineers, and bring them back to England for trial and punishment. The Pandora reached Tahiti March 23, 1791, set sail, with fourteen prisoners, May 8, and was wrecked on the "Great Barrier Reef" north-east of Queensland, August 29, 1791. Four of the prisoners, including George Stewart, who had been manacled, and were confined in "Pandora's box," perished in the wreck, and the remaining ten were brought back to England, and tried by court-martial. (See The Eventful History of the Mutiny, etc. (by Sir John Barrow), 1831, pp. 205-244.)

The story, which runs through the second, third, and fourth cantos, may possibly owe some of its details to a vague recollection of incidents which happened, or were supposed to happen, at Tahiti, in the interval between the final departure of the Bounty, September 21, 1789, and the arrival of the Pandora, March 23, 1791; but, as a whole, it is a work of fiction.

With the exception of the fifteenth and sixteenth cantos of Don Juan, The Island was the last poem of any importance which Byron lived to write, and the question naturally suggests itself—Is the new song as good as the old? Byron answers the question himself. He tells Leigh Hunt (January 25, 1823) that he hopes the "poem will be a little above the ordinary run of periodical poesy," and that, though portions of the Toobonai (sic) islanders are "pamby," he intends "to scatter some uncommon places here and there nevertheless." On the whole, in point of conception and execution, The Island is weaker and less coherent than the Corsair; but it contains lines and passages (e.g. Canto I. lines

107-124, 133-140; Canto II. lines 272-297; Canto IV. lines 94-188) which display a finer feeling and a more "exalted wit" than the "purple patches" of The Turkish Tales.

The poetic faculty is somewhat exhausted, but the poetic vision has been purged and heightened by suffering and self-knowledge.

The Island was reviewed in the Monthly Review, July, 1823, E.S., vol. 101, pp. 316-319; the New Monthly Magazine, N.S., 1823, vol. 8, pp. 136-141; the Atlantic Magazine, April, 1826, vol. 2, pp. 333-337; in the Literary Chronicle, June 21, 1823; and the Literary Gazette, June 21, 1823.

ADVERTISEMENT.

The foundation of the following story will be found partly in Lieutenant Bligh's "Narrative of the Mutiny and Seizure of the Bounty, in the South Seas (in 1789);" and partly in "Mariner's Account of the Tonga Islands."

GENOA, 1823.

THE ISLAND

CANTO THE FIRST.

I.

The morning watch was come; the vessel lay
Her course, and gently made her liquid way;
The cloven billow flashed from off her prow
In furrows formed by that majestic plough;
The waters with their world were all before;
Behind, the South Sea's many an islet shore.
The quiet night, now dappling, 'gan to wane,
Dividing darkness from the dawning main;
The dolphins, not unconscious of the day,
Swam high, as eager of the coming ray;
The stars from broader beams began to creep,
And lift their shining eyelids from the deep;
The sail resumed its lately shadowed white,
And the wind fluttered with a freshening flight;
The purpling Ocean owns the coming Sun,
But ere he break—a deed is to be done.

II.

The gallant Chief within his cabin slept,

Secure in those by whom the watch was kept:
His dreams were of Old England's welcome shore,
Of toils rewarded, and of dangers o'er;
His name was added to the glorious roll
Of those who search the storm-surrounded Pole.
The worst was over, and the rest seemed sure,
And why should not his slumber be secure?
Alas! his deck was trod by unwilling feet,
And wilder hands would hold the vessel's sheet;
Young hearts, which languished for some sunny isle,
Where summer years and summer women smile;
Men without country, who, too long estranged,
Had found no native home, or found it changed,
And, half uncivilised, preferred the cave
Of some soft savage to the uncertain wave—
The gushing fruits that nature gave unfilled;
The wood without a path — but where they willed;
The field o'er which promiscuous Plenty poured
Her horn; the equal land without a lord;
The wish—which ages have not yet subdued
In man—to have no master save his mood;
The earth, whose mine was on its face, unsold,
The glowing sun and produce all its gold;
The Freedom which can call each grot a home;
The general garden, where all steps may roam,
Where Nature owns a nation as her child,
Exulting in the enjoyment of the wild;
Their shells, their fruits, the only wealth they know,
Their unexploring navy, the canoe;
Their sport, the dashing breakers and the chase;
Their strangest sight, an European face:—
Such was the country which these strangers yearned
To see again—a sight they dearly earned.

III.

Awake, bold Bligh! the foe is at the gate!
Awake! awake!—Alas! it is too late!
Fiercely beside thy cot the mutineer
Stands, and proclaims the reign of rage and fear.
Thy limbs are bound, the bayonet at thy breast;
The hands, which trembled at thy voice, arrest;
Dragged o'er the deck, no more at thy command
The obedient helm shall veer, the sail expand;
That savage Spirit, which would lull by wrath
Its desperate escape from Duty's path,
Glares round thee, in the scarce believing eyes
Of those who fear the Chief they sacrifice:
For ne'er can Man his conscience all assuage,
Unless he drain the wine of Passion—Rage.

IV.

In vain, not silenced by the eye of Death,
Thou call'st the loyal with thy menaced breath:—
They come not; they are few, and, overawed,
Must acquiesce, while sterner hearts applaud.
In vain thou dost demand the cause: a curse
Is all the answer, with the threat of worse.
Full in thine eyes is waved the glittering blade,
Close to thy throat the pointed bayonet laid.
The levelled muskets circle round thy breast
In hands as steeled to do the deadly rest.
Thou dar'st them to their worst, exclaiming—"Fire!"
But they who pitied not could yet admire;
Some lurking remnant of their former awe
Restrained them longer than their broken law;
They would not dip their souls at once in blood,
But left thee to the mercies of the flood.

V.

"Hoist out the boat!" was now the leader's cry;
And who dare answer "No!" to Mutiny,
In the first dawning of the drunken hour,
The Saturnalia of unhoped-for power?
The boat is lowered with all the haste of hate,
With its slight plank between thee and thy fate,
Her only cargo such a scant supply
As promises the death their hands deny;
And just enough of water and of bread
To keep, some days, the dying from the dead:
Some cordage, canvass, sails, and lines, and twine,
But treasures all to hermits of the brine,
Were added after, to the earnest prayer
Of those who saw no hope, save sea and air;
And last, that trembling vassal of the Pole—
The feeling compass—Navigation's soul.

VI.

And now the self-elected Chief finds time
To stun the first sensation of his crime,
And raise it in his followers—"Ho! the bowl!"
Lest passion should return to reason's shoal.
"Brandy for heroes!" Burke could once exclaim—
No doubt a liquid path to Epic fame;
And such the new-born heroes found it here,

And drained the draught with an applauding cheer.
"Huzza! for Otaheite!" was the cry.
How strange such shouts from sons of Mutiny!
The gentle island, and the genial soil,
The friendly hearts, the feasts without a toil,
The courteous manners but from nature caught,
The wealth unhoarded, and the love unbought;
Could these have charms for rudest sea-boys, driven
Before the mast by every wind of heaven?
And now, even now prepared with others' woes
To earn mild Virtue's vain desire, repose?
Alas! such is our nature! all but aim
At the same end by pathways not the same;
Our means—our birth—our nation, and our name,
Our fortune—temper—even our outward frame,
Are far more potent o'er our yielding clay
Than aught we know beyond our little day.
Yet still there whispers the small voice within,
Heard through Gain's silence, and o'er Glory's din:
Whatever creed be taught, or land be trod,
Man's conscience is the Oracle of God.

VII.

The launch is crowded with the faithful few
Who wait their Chief, a melancholy crew:
But some remained reluctant on the deck
Of that proud vessel—now a moral wreck—
And viewed their Captain's fate with piteous eyes;
While others scoffed his augured miseries,
Sneered at the prospect of his pigmy sail,
And the slight bark so laden and so frail.
The tender nautilus, who steers his prow,
The sea-born sailor of his shell canoe,
The ocean Mab, the fairy of the sea,
Seems far less fragile, and, alas! more free.
He, when the lightning-winged Tornados sweep
The surge, is safe—his port is in the deep—
And triumphs o'er the armadas of Mankind,
Which shake the World, yet crumble in the wind.

VIII.

When all was now prepared, the vessel clear
Which hailed her master in the mutineer,
A seaman, less obdurate than his mates,
Showed the vain pity which but irritates;
Watched his late Chieftain with exploring eye,
And told, in signs, repentant sympathy;

Held the moist shaddock to his parched mouth,
Which felt Exhaustion's deep and bitter drouth.
But soon observed, this guardian was withdrawn,
Nor further Mercy clouds Rebellion's dawn.
Then forward stepped the bold and froward boy
His Chief had cherished only to destroy,
And, pointing to the helpless prow beneath,
Exclaimed, "Depart at once! delay is death!"
Yet then, even then, his feelings ceased not all:
In that last moment could a word recall
Remorse for the black deed as yet half done,
And what he hid from many showed to one:
When Bligh in stern reproach demanded where
Was now his grateful sense of former care?
Where all his hopes to see his name aspire,
And blazon Britain's thousand glories higher?
His feverish lips thus broke their gloomy spell,
"Tis that! 'tis that! I am in hell! in hell!"
No more he said; but urging to the bark
His Chief, commits him to his fragile ark;
These the sole accents from his tongue that fell,
But volumes lurked below his fierce farewell.

IX.

The arctic Sun rose broad above the wave;
The breeze now sank, now whispered from his cave;
As on the Æolian harp, his fitful wings
Now swelled, now fluttered o'er his Ocean strings.
With slow, despairing oar, the abandoned skiff
Ploughs its drear progress to the scarce seen cliff,
Which lifts its peak a cloud above the main:
That boat and ship shall never meet again!

But 'tis not mine to tell their tale of grief,
Their constant peril, and their scant relief;
Their days of danger, and their nights of pain;
Their manly courage even when deemed in vain;
The sapping famine, rendering scarce a son
Known to his mother in the skeleton;
The ills that lessened still their little store,
And starved even Hunger till he wrung no more;
The varying frowns and favours of the deep,
That now almost ingulfs, then leaves to creep
With crazy oar and shattered strength along
The tide that yields reluctant to the strong;
The incessant fever of that arid thirst
Which welcomes, as a well, the clouds that burst
Above their naked bones, and feels delight

In the cold drenching of the stormy night,
And from the outspread canvass gladly wrings
A drop to moisten Life's all-gasping springs;
The savage foe escaped, to seek again
More hospitable shelter from the main;
The ghastly Spectres which were doomed at last
To tell as true a tale of dangers past,
As ever the dark annals of the deep
Disclosed for man to dread or woman weep.

X.

We leave them to their fate, but not unknown
Nor unredressed. Revenge may have her own:
Roused Discipline aloud proclaims their cause,
And injured Navies urge their broken laws.
Pursue we on his track the mutineer,
Whom distant vengeance had not taught to fear.
Wide o'er the wave—away! away! away!
Once more his eyes shall hail the welcome bay;
Once more the happy shores without a law
Receive the outlaws whom they lately saw;
Nature, and Nature's goddess—Woman—woos
To lands where, save their conscience, none accuse;
Where all partake the earth without dispute,
And bread itself is gathered as a fruit;
Where none contest the fields, the woods, the streams:—
The goldless Age, where Gold disturbs no dreams,
Inhabits or inhabited the shore,
Till Europe taught them better than before;
Bestowed her customs, and amended theirs,
But left her vices also to their heirs.
Away with this! behold them as they were,
Do good with Nature, or with Nature err.
"Huzza! for Otaheite!" was the cry,
As stately swept the gallant vessel by.
The breeze springs up; the lately flapping sail
Extends its arch before the growing gale;
In swifter ripples stream aside the seas,
Which her bold bow flings off with dashing ease.
Thus Argo ploughed the Euxine's virgin foam,
But those she wafted still looked back to home;
These spurn their country with their rebel bark,
And fly her as the raven fled the Ark;
And yet they seek to nestle with the dove,
And tame their fiery spirits down to Love.

I.

How pleasant were the songs of Toobonai,
When Summer's Sun went down the coral bay!
Come, let us to the islet's softest shade,
And hear the warbling birds! the damsels said:
The wood-dove from the forest depth shall coo,
Like voices of the Gods from Bolotoo;
We'll cull the flowers that grow above the dead,
For these most bloom where rests the warrior's head;
And we will sit in Twilight's face, and see
The sweet Moon glancing through the Tooa tree,
The lofty accents of whose sighing bough
Shall sadly please us as we lean below;
Or climb the steep, and view the surf in vain
Wrestle with rocky giants o'er the main,
Which spurn in columns back the baffled spray.
How beautiful are these! how happy they,
Who, from the toil and tumult of their lives,
Steal to look down where nought but Ocean strives!
Even He too loves at times the blue lagoon,
And smooths his ruffled mane beneath the Moon.

II.

Yes—from the sepulchre we'll gather flowers,
Then feast like spirits in their promised bowers,
Then plunge and revel in the rolling surf,
Then lay our limbs along the tender turf,
And, wet and shining from the sportive toil,
Anoint our bodies with the fragrant oil,
And plait our garlands gathered from the grave,
And wear the wreaths that sprung from out the brave.
But lo! night comes, the Mooa woos us back,
The sound of mats are heard along our track;
Anon the torchlight dance shall fling its sheen
In flashing mazes o'er the Marly's green;
And we too will be there; we too recall
The memory bright with many a festival,
Ere Fiji blew the shell of war, when foes
For the first time were wafted in canoes.
Alas! for them the flower of manhood bleeds;
Alas! for them our fields are rank with weeds:
Forgotten is the rapture, or unknown,
Of wandering with the Moon and Love alone.
But be it so:—they taught us how to wield
The club, and rain our arrows o'er the field:
Now let them reap the harvest of their art!

But feast to-night! to-morrow we depart.
Strike up the dance! the Cava bowl fill high!
Drain every drop!—to-morrow we may die.
In summer garments be our limbs arrayed;
Around our waists the Tappa's white displayed;
Thick wreaths shall form our coronal, like Spring's,
And round our necks shall glance the Hooni strings;
So shall their brighter hues contrast the glow
Of the dusk bosoms that beat high below.

III.

But now the dance is o'er—yet stay awhile;
Ah, pause! nor yet put out the social smile.
To-morrow for the Mooa we depart,
But not to-night—to-night is for the heart.
Again bestow the wreaths we gently woo,
Ye young Enchantresses of gay Licoo!
How lovely are your forms! how every sense
Bows to your beauties, softened, but intense,
Like to the flowers on Mataloco's steep,
Which fling their fragrance far athwart the deep!—
We too will see Licoo; but—oh! my heart!—
What do I say?—to-morrow we depart!

IV.

Thus rose a song—the harmony of times
Before the winds blew Europe o'er these climes.
True, they had vices—such are Nature's growth—
But only the barbarian's—we have both;
The sordor of civilisation, mixed
With all the savage which Man's fall hath fixed.
Who hath not seen Dissimulation's reign,
The prayers of Abel linked to deeds of Cain?
Who such would see may from his lattice view
The Old World more degraded than the New,—
Now new no more, save where Columbia rears
Twin giants, born by Freedom to her spheres,
Where Chimborazo, over air,—earth,—wave,—
Glares with his Titan eye, and sees no slave.

V.

Such was this ditty of Tradition's days,
Which to the dead a lingering fame conveys
In song, where Fame as yet hath left no sign
Beyond the sound whose charm is half divine;

Which leaves no record to the sceptic eye,
But yields young History all to Harmony;
A boy Achilles, with the Centaur's lyre
In hand, to teach him to surpass his sire.
For one long-cherished ballad's simple stave,
Rung from the rock, or mingled with the wave,
Or from the bubbling streamlet's grassy side,
Or gathering mountain echoes as they glide,
Hath greater power o'er each true heart and ear,
Than all the columns Conquest's minions rear;
Invites, when Hieroglyphics are a theme
For sages' labours, or the student's dream;
Attracts, when History's volumes are a toil,—
The first, the freshest bud of Feeling's soil.
Such was this rude rhyme—rhyme is of the rude—
But such inspired the Norseman's solitude,
Who came and conquered; such, wherever rise
Lands which no foes destroy or civilise,
Exist: and what can our accomplished art
Of verse do more than reach the awakened heart?

VI.

And sweetly now those untaught melodies
Broke the luxurious silence of the skies,
The sweet siesta of a summer day,
The tropic afternoon of Toobonai,
When every flower was bloom, and air was balm,
And the first breath began to stir the palm,
The first yet voiceless wind to urge the wave
All gently to refresh the thirsty cave,
Where sat the Songstress with the stranger boy,
Who taught her Passion's desolating joy,
Too powerful over every heart, but most
O'er those who know not how it may be lost;
O'er those who, burning in the new-born fire,
Like martyrs revel in their funeral pyre,
With such devotion to their ecstacy,
That Life knows no such rapture as to die:
And die they do; for earthly life has nought
Matched with that burst of Nature, even in thought;
And all our dreams of better life above
But close in one eternal gush of Love.

VII.

There sat the gentle savage of the wild,
In growth a woman, though in years a child,
As childhood dates within our colder clime,

Where nought is ripened rapidly save crime;
The infant of an infant world, as pure
From Nature—lovely, warm, and premature;
Dusky like night, but night with all her stars;
Or cavern sparkling with its native spars;
With eyes that were a language and a spell,
A form like Aphrodite's in her shell,
With all her loves around her on the deep,
Voluptuous as the first approach of sleep;
Yet full of life—for through her tropic cheek
The blush would make its way, and all but speak;
The sun-born blood suffused her neck, and threw
O'er her clear nut-brown skin a lucid hue,
Like coral reddening through the darkened wave,
Which draws the diver to the crimson cave.
Such was this daughter of the southern seas,
Herself a billow in her energies,
To bear the bark of others' happiness,
Nor feel a sorrow till their joy grew less:
Her wild and warm yet faithful bosom knew
No joy like what it gave; her hopes ne'er drew
Aught from Experience, that chill touchstone, whose
Sad proof reduces all things from their hues:
She feared no ill, because she knew it not,
Or what she knew was soon—too soon—forgot:
Her smiles and tears had passed, as light winds pass
O'er lakes to ruffle, not destroy, their glass,
Whose depths unsearched, and fountains from the hill,
Restore their surface, in itself so still,
Until the Earthquake tear the Naiad's cave,
Root up the spring, and trample on the wave,
And crush the living waters to a mass,
The amphibious desert of the dank morass!
And must their fate be hers? The eternal change
But grasps Humanity with quicker range;
And they who fall but fall as worlds will fall,
To rise, if just, a Spirit o'er them all.

VIII.

And who is he? the blue-eyed northern child
Of isles more known to man, but scarce less wild;
The fair-haired offspring of the Hebrides,
Where roars the Pentland with its whirling seas;
Rocked in his cradle by the roaring wind,
The tempest-born in body and in mind,
His young eyes opening on the ocean-foam,
Had from that moment deemed the deep his home,
The giant comrade of his pensive moods,
The sharer of his craggy solitudes,

The only Mentor of his youth, where'er
His bark was borne; the sport of wave and air;
A careless thing, who placed his choice in chance,
Nursed by the legends of his land's romance;
Eager to hope, but not less firm to bear,
Acquainted with all feelings save despair.
Placed in the Arab's clime he would have been
As bold a rover as the sands have seen,
And braved their thirst with as enduring lip
As Ishmael, wafted on his Desert-Ship;
Fixed upon Chili's shore, a proud cacique:
On Hellas' mountains, a rebellious Greek;
Born in a tent, perhaps a Tamerlane;
Bred to a throne, perhaps unfit to reign.
For the same soul that rends its path to sway,
If reared to such, can find no further prey
Beyond itself, and must retrace its way,
Plunging for pleasure into pain: the same
Spirit which made a Nero, Rome's worst shame,
A humbler state and discipline of heart,
Had formed his glorious namesake's counterpart;
But grant his vices, grant them all his own,
How small their theatre without a throne!

IX.

Thou smilest:—these comparisons seem high
To those who scan all things with dazzled eye;
Linked with the unknown name of one whose doom
Has nought to do with glory or with Rome,
With Chili, Hellas, or with Araby;—
Thou smilest?—Smile; 'tis better thus than sigh;
Yet such he might have been; he was a man,
A soaring spirit, ever in the van,
A patriot hero or despotic chief,
To form a nation's glory or its grief,
Born under auspices which make us more
Or less than we delight to ponder o'er.
But these are visions; say, what was he here?
A blooming boy, a truant mutineer.
The fair-haired Torquil, free as Ocean's spray,
The husband of the bride of Toobonai.

X.

By Neuha's side he sate, and watched the waters,—
Neuha, the sun-flower of the island daughters,
Highborn, (a birth at which the herald smiles,
Without a scutcheon for these secret isles,)

Of a long race, the valiant and the free,
The naked knights of savage chivalry,
Whose grassy cairns ascend along the shore;
And thine—I've seen—Achilles! do no more.
She, when the thunder-bearing strangers came,
In vast canoes, begirt with bolts of flame,
Topped with tall trees, which, loftier than the palm,
Seemed rooted in the deep amidst its calm:
But when the winds awakened, shot forth wings
Broad as the cloud along the horizon flings,
And swayed the waves, like cities of the sea,
Making the very billows look less free;—
She, with her paddling oar and dancing prow,
Shot through the surf, like reindeer through the snow,
Swift-gliding o'er the breaker's whitening edge,
Light as a Nereid in her ocean sledge,
And gazed and wondered at the giant hulk,
Which heaved from wave to wave its trampling bulk.
The anchor dropped; it lay along the deep,
Like a huge lion in the sun asleep,
While round it swarmed the Proas' flitting chain,
Like summer bees that hum around his mane.

XI.

The white man landed!—need the rest be told?
The New World stretched its dusk hand to the Old;
Each was to each a marvel, and the tie
Of wonder warmed to better sympathy.
Kind was the welcome of the sun-born sires,
And kinder still their daughters' gentler fires.
Their union grew: the children of the storm
Found beauty linked with many a dusky form;
While these in turn admired the paler glow,
Which seemed so white in climes that knew no snow.
The chace, the race, the liberty to roam,
The soil where every cottage showed a home;
The sea-spread net, the lightly launched canoe,
Which stemmed the studded archipelago,
O'er whose blue bosom rose the starry isles;
The healthy slumber, earned by sportive toils;
The palm, the loftiest Dryad of the woods,
Within whose bosom infant Bacchus broods,
While eagles scarce build higher than the crest
Which shadows o'er the vineyard in her breast;
The Cava feast, the Yam, the Cocoa's root,
Which bears at once the cup, and milk, and fruit;
The Bread-tree, which, without the ploughshare, yields
The unreaped harvest of unfurrowed fields,
And bakes its unadulterated loaves

Without a furnace in unpurchased groves,
And flings off famine from its fertile breast,
A priceless market for the gathering guest;—
These, with the luxuries of seas and woods,
The airy joys of social solitudes,
Tamed each rude wanderer to the sympathies
Of those who were more happy, if less wise,
Did more than Europe's discipline had done,
And civilised Civilisation's son!

XII.

Of these, and there was many a willing pair,
Neuha and Torquil were not the least fair:
Both children of the isles, though distant far;
Both born beneath a sea-presiding star;
Both nourished amidst Nature's native scenes,
Loved to the last, whatever intervenes
Between us and our Childhood's sympathy,
Which still reverts to what first caught the eye.
He who first met the Highlands' swelling blue
Will love each peak that shows a kindred hue,
Hail in each crag a friend's familiar face,
And clasp the mountain in his Mind's embrace.
Long have I roamed through lands which are not mine,
Adored the Alp, and loved the Apennine,
Revered Parnassus, and beheld the steep
Jove's Ida and Olympus crown the deep:
But 'twas not all long ages' lore, nor all
Their nature held me in their thrilling thrall;
The infant rapture still survived the boy,
And Loch-na-gar with Ida looked o'er Troy,
Mixed Celtic memories with the Phrygian mount,
And Highland linns with Castalie's clear fount.
Forgive me, Homer's universal shade!
Forgive me, Phœbus! that my fancy strayed;
The North and Nature taught me to adore
Your scenes sublime, from those beloved before.

XIII.

The love which maketh all things fond and fair,
The youth which makes one rainbow of the air,
The dangers past, that make even Man enjoy
The pause in which he ceases to destroy,
The mutual beauty, which the sternest feel
Strike to their hearts like lightning to the steel,
United the half savage and the whole,
The maid and boy, in one absorbing soul.

No more the thundering memory of the fight
Wrapped his weaned bosom in its dark delight;
No more the irksome restlessness of Rest
Disturbed him like the eagle in her nest,
Whose whetted beak and far-pervading eye
Darts for a victim over all the sky:
His heart was tamed to that voluptuous state,
At once Elysian and effeminate,
Which leaves no laurels o'er the Hero's urn;—
These wither when for aught save blood they burn;
Yet when their ashes in their nook are laid,
Doth not the myrtle leave as sweet a shade?
Had Cæsar known but Cleopatra's kiss,
Rome had been free, the world had not been his.
And what have Cæsar's deeds and Cæsar's fame
Done for the earth? We feel them in our shame.
The gory sanction of his Glory stains
The rust which tyrants cherish on our chains.
Though Glory—Nature—Reason—Freedom, bid
Roused millions do what single Brutus did—
Sweep these mere mock-birds of the Despot's song
From the tall bough where they have perched so long,—
Still are we hawked at by such mousing owls,
And take for falcons those ignoble fowls,
When but a word of freedom would dispel
These bugbears, as their terrors show too well.

XIV.

Rapt in the fond forgetfulness of life,
Neuha, the South Sea girl, was all a wife,
With no distracting world to call her off
From Love; with no Society to scoff
At the new transient flame; no babbling crowd
Of coxcombry in admiration loud,
Or with adulterous whisper to alloy
Her duty, and her glory, and her joy:
With faith and feelings naked as her form,
She stood as stands a rainbow in a storm,
Changing its hues with bright variety,
But still expanding lovelier o'er the sky,
Howe'er its arch may swell, its colours move,
The cloud-compelling harbinger of Love.

XV.

Here, in this grotto of the wave-worn shore,
They passed the Tropic's red meridian o'er;
Nor long the hours—they never paused o'er time,

Unbroken by the clock's funereal chime,
Which deals the daily pittance of our span,
And points and mocks with iron laugh at man.
What deemed they of the future or the past?
The present, like a tyrant, held them fast:
Their hour-glass was the sea-sand, and the tide,
Like her smooth billow, saw their moments glide
Their clock the Sun, in his unbounded tower
They reckoned not, whose day was but an hour;
The nightingale, their only vesper-bell,
Sung sweetly to the rose the day's farewell;
The broad Sun set, but not with lingering sweep,
As in the North he mellows o'er the deep;
But fiery, full, and fierce, as if he left
The World for ever, earth of light bereft,
Plunged with red forehead down along the wave,
As dives a hero headlong to his grave.
Then rose they, looking first along the skies,
And then for light into each other's eyes,
Wondering that Summer showed so brief a sun,
And asking if indeed the day were done.

XVI.

And let not this seem strange: the devotee
Lives not in earth, but in his ecstasy;
Around him days and worlds are heedless driven,
His Soul is gone before his dust to Heaven.
Is Love less potent? No—his path is trod,
Alike uplifted gloriously to God;
Or linked to all we know of Heaven below,
The other better self, whose joy or woe
Is more than ours; the all-absorbing flame
Which, kindled by another, grows the same,
Wrapt in one blaze; the pure, yet funeral pile,
Where gentle hearts, like Bramins, sit and smile.
How often we forget all time, when lone,
Admiring Nature's universal throne,
Her woods—her wilds—her waters—the intense
Reply of hers to our intelligence!
Live not the Stars and Mountains? Are the Waves
Without a spirit? Are the dropping caves
Without a feeling in their silent tears?
No, no;—they woo and clasp us to their spheres,
Dissolve this clog and clod of clay before
Its hour, and merge our soul in the great shore.
Strip off this fond and false identity!
Who thinks of self when gazing on the sky?
And who, though gazing lower, ever thought,
In the young moments ere the heart is taught

Time's lesson, of Man's baseness or his own?
All Nature is his realm, and Love his throne.

XVII.

Neuha arose, and Torquil: Twilight's hour
Came sad and softly to their rocky bower,
Which, kindling by degrees its dewy spars,
Echoed their dim light to the mustering stars.
Slowly the pair, partaking Nature's calm,
Sought out their cottage, built beneath the palm;
Now smiling and now silent, as the scene;
Lovely as Love—the Spirit!—when serene.
The Ocean scarce spoke louder with his swell,
Than breathes his mimic murmurer in the shell,
As, far divided from his parent deep,
The sea-born infant cries, and will not sleep,
Raising his little plaint in vain, to rave
For the broad bosom of his nursing wave:
The woods drooped darkly, as inclined to rest,
The tropic bird wheeled rockward to his nest,
And the blue sky spread round them like a lake
Of peace, where Piety her thirst might slake.

XVIII.

But through the palm and plantain, hark, a Voice!
Not such as would have been a lover's choice,
In such an hour, to break the air so still;
No dying night-breeze, harping o'er the hill,
Striking the strings of nature, rock and tree,
Those best and earliest lyres of Harmony,
With Echo for their chorus; nor the alarm
Of the loud war-whoop to dispel the charm;
Nor the soliloquy of the hermit owl,
Exhaling all his solitary soul,
The dim though large-eyed wingéd anchorite,
Who peals his dreary Pæan o'er the night;
But a loud, long, and naval whistle, shrill
As ever started through a sea-bird's bill;
And then a pause, and then a hoarse "Hillo!
Torquil, my boy! what cheer? Ho! brother, ho!"
"Who hails?" cried Torquil, following with his eye
The sound. "Here's one," was all the brief reply.

XIX.

But here the herald of the self-same mouth
Came breathing o'er the aromatic south,
Not like a "bed of violets" on the gale,
But such as wafts its cloud o'er grog or ale,
Borne from a short frail pipe, which yet had blown
Its gentle odours over either zone,
And, puffed where'er winds rise or waters roll,
Had wafted smoke from Portsmouth to the Pole,
Opposed its vapour as the lightning flashed,
And reeked, 'midst mountain-billows, unabashed,
To Æolus a constant sacrifice,
Through every change of all the varying skies.
And what was he who bore it?—I may err,
But deem him sailor or philosopher.
Sublime Tobacco! which from East to West
Cheers the tar's labour or the Turkman's rest;
Which on the Moslem's ottoman divides
His hours, and rivals opium and his brides;
Magnificent in Stamboul, but less grand,
Though not less loved, in Wapping or the Strand;
Divine in hookas, glorious in a pipe,
When tipped with amber, mellow, rich, and ripe:
Like other charmers, wooing the caress,
More dazzlingly when daring in full dress;
Yet thy true lovers more admire by far
Thy naked beauties—Give me a cigar!

XX.

Through the approaching darkness of the wood
A human figure broke the solitude,
Fantastically, it may be, arrayed,
A seaman in a savage masquerade;
Such as appears to rise out from the deep,
When o'er the line the merry vessels sweep,
And the rough Saturnalia of the tar
Flock o'er the deck, in Neptune's borrowed car;
And, pleased, the God of Ocean sees his name
Revive once more, though but in mimic game
Of his true sons, who riot in the breeze
Undreamt of in his native Cyclades.
Still the old God delights, from out the main,
To snatch some glimpses of his ancient reign.
Our sailor's jacket, though in ragged trim,
His constant pipe, which never yet burned dim,
His foremast air, and somewhat rolling gait,
Like his dear vessel, spoke his former state;
But then a sort of kerchief round his head,
Not over tightly bound, nor nicely spread;

And, 'stead of trowsers (ah! too early torn!
For even the mildest woods will have their thorn)
A curious sort of somewhat scanty mat
Now served for inexpressibles and hat;
His naked feet and neck, and sunburnt face,
Perchance might suit alike with either race.
His arms were all his own, our Europe's growth,
Which two worlds bless for civilising both;
The musket swung behind his shoulders broad,
And somewhat stooped by his marine abode,
But brawny as the boar's; and hung beneath,
His cutlass drooped, unconscious of a sheath,
Or lost or worn away; his pistols were
Linked to his belt, a matrimonial pair—
(Let not this metaphor appear a scoff,
Though one missed fire, the other would go off);
These, with a bayonet, not so free from rust
As when the arm-chest held its brighter trust,
Completed his accoutrements, as Night
Surveyed him in his garb heteroclite.

XXI.

"What cheer, Ben Bunting?" cried (when in full view
Our new acquaintance) Torquil. "Aught of new?"
"Ey, ey!" quoth Ben, "not new, but news enow;
A strange sail in the offing."—"Sail! and how?
What! could you make her out? It cannot be;
I've seen no rag of canvass on the sea."
"Belike," said Ben, "you might not from the bay,
But from the bluff-head, where I watched to-day,
I saw her in the doldrums; for the wind
Was light and baffling."—"When the Sun declined
Where lay she? had she anchored?"—"No, but still
She bore down on us, till the wind grew still."
"Her flag?"—"I had no glass: but fore and aft,
Egad! she seemed a wicked-looking craft."
"Armed?"—"I expect so;—sent on the look-out:
'Tis time, belike, to put our helm about."
"About?—Whate'er may have us now in chase,
We'll make no running fight, for that were base;
We will die at our quarters, like true men."
"Ey, ey! for that 'tis all the same to Ben."
"Does Christian know this?"—"Aye; he has piped all hands
To quarters. They are furbishing the stands
Of arms; and we have got some guns to bear,
And scaled them. You are wanted."—"That's but fair;
And if it were not, mine is not the soul
To leave my comrades helpless on the shoal.
My Neuha! ah! and must my fate pursue

Not me alone, but one so sweet and true?
But whatsoe'er betide, ah, Neuha! now
Unman me not: the hour will not allow
A tear; I am thine whatever intervenes!"
"Right," quoth Ben; "that will do for the marines."

CANTO THE THIRD.

I.

The fight was o'er; the flashing through the gloom,
Which robes the cannon as he wings a tomb,
Had ceased; and sulphury vapours upward driven
Had left the Earth, and but polluted Heaven:
The rattling roar which rung in every volley
Had left the echoes to their melancholy;
No more they shrieked their horror, boom for boom;
The strife was done, the vanquished had their doom;
The mutineers were crushed, dispersed, or ta'en,
Or lived to deem the happiest were the slain.
Few, few escaped, and these were hunted o'er
The isle they loved beyond their native shore.
No further home was theirs, it seemed, on earth,
Once renegades to that which gave them birth;
Tracked like wild beasts, like them they sought the wild,
As to a Mother's bosom flies the child;
But vainly wolves and lions seek their den,
And still more vainly men escape from men.

II.

Beneath a rock whose jutting base protrudes
Far over Ocean in its fiercest moods,
When scaling his enormous crag the wave
Is hurled down headlong, like the foremost brave,
And falls back on the foaming crowd behind,
Which fight beneath the banners of the wind,
But now at rest, a little remnant drew
Together, bleeding, thirsty, faint, and few;
But still their weapons in their hands, and still
With something of the pride of former will,
As men not all unused to meditate,
And strive much more than wonder at their fate.
Their present lot was what they had foreseen,
And dared as what was likely to have been;
Yet still the lingering hope, which deemed their lot
Not pardoned, but unsought for or forgot,

Or trusted that, if sought, their distant caves
Might still be missed amidst the world of waves,
Had weaned their thoughts in part from what they saw
And felt, the vengeance of their country's law.
Their sea-green isle, their guilt-won Paradise,
No more could shield their Virtue or their Vice:
Their better feelings, if such were, were thrown
Back on themselves,—their sins remained alone.
Proscribed even in their second country, they
Were lost; in vain the World before them lay;
All outlets seemed secured. Their new allies
Had fought and bled in mutual sacrifice;
But what availed the club and spear, and arm
Of Hercules, against the sulphury charm,
The magic of the thunder, which destroyed
The warrior ere his strength could be employed?
Dug, like a spreading pestilence, the grave
No less of human bravery than the brave!
Their own scant numbers acted all the few
Against the many oft will dare and do;
But though the choice seems native to die free,
Even Greece can boast but one Thermopylæ,
Till now, when she has forged her broken chain
Back to a sword, and dies and lives again!

III.

Beside the jutting rock the few appeared,
Like the last remnant of the red-deer's herd;
Their eyes were feverish, and their aspect worn,
But still the hunter's blood was on their horn.
A little stream came tumbling from the height,
And straggling into ocean as it might,
Its bounding crystal frolicked in the ray,
And gushed from cliff to crag with saltless spray;
Close on the wild, wide ocean, yet as pure
And fresh as Innocence, and more secure,
Its silver torrent glittered o'er the deep,
As the shy chamois' eye o'erlooks the steep,
While far below the vast and sullen swell
Of Ocean's alpine azure rose and fell.
To this young spring they rushed,—all feelings first
Absorbed in Passion's and in Nature's thirst,—
Drank as they do who drink their last, and threw
Their arms aside to revel in its dew;
Cooled their scorched throats, and washed the gory stains
From wounds whose only bandage might be chains;
Then, when their drought was quenched, looked sadly round,
As wondering how so many still were found

Alive and fetterless:—but silent all,
Each sought his fellow's eyes, as if to call
On him for language which his lips denied,
As though their voices with their cause had died.

IV.

Stern, and aloof a little from the rest,
Stood Christian, with his arms across his chest.
The ruddy, reckless, dauntless hue once spread
Along his cheek was livid now as lead;
His light-brown locks, so graceful in their flow,
Now rose like startled vipers o'er his brow.
Still as a statue, with his lips comprest
To stifle even the breath within his breast,
Fast by the rock, all menacing, but mute,
He stood; and, save a slight beat of his foot,
Which deepened now and then the sandy dint
Beneath his heel, his form seemed turned to flint.
Some paces further Torquil leaned his head
Against a bank, and spoke not, but he bled,—
Not mortally:—his worst wound was within;
His brow was pale, his blue eyes sunken in,
And blood-drops, sprinkled o'er his yellow hair,
Showed that his faintness came not from despair,
But Nature's ebb. Beside him was another,
Rough as a bear, but willing as a brother,—
Ben Bunting, who essayed to wash, and wipe,
And bind his wound—then calmly lit his pipe,
A trophy which survived a hundred fights,
A beacon which had cheered ten thousand nights.
The fourth and last of this deserted group
Walked up and down—at times would stand, then stoop
To pick a pebble up—then let it drop—
Then hurry as in haste—then quickly stop—
Then cast his eyes on his companions—then
Half whistle half a tune, and pause again—
And then his former movements would redouble,
With something between carelessness and trouble.
This is a long description, but applies
To scarce five minutes passed before the eyes;
But yet what minutes! Moments like to these
Rend men's lives into immortalities.

V.

At length Jack Skyscrape, a mercurial man,
Who fluttered over all things like a fan,
More brave than firm, and more disposed to dare

And die at once than wrestle with despair,
Exclaimed, "G—d damn!"—those syllables intense,—
Nucleus of England's native eloquence,
As the Turk's "Allah!" or the Roman's more
Pagan "Proh Jupiter!" was wont of yore
To give their first impressions such a vent,
By way of echo to embarrassment.
Jack was embarrassed,—never hero more,
And as he knew not what to say, he swore:
Nor swore in vain; the long congenial sound
Revived Ben Bunting from his pipe profound;
He drew it from his mouth, and looked full wise,
But merely added to the oath his eyes;
Thus rendering the imperfect phrase complete,
A peroration I need not repeat.

VI.

But Christian, of a higher order, stood
Like an extinct volcano in his mood;
Silent, and sad, and savage,—with the trace
Of passion reeking from his clouded face;
Till lifting up again his sombre eye,
It glanced on Torquil, who leaned faintly by.
"And is it thus?" he cried, "unhappy boy!
And thee, too, thee—my madness must destroy!"
He said, and strode to where young Torquil stood,
Yet dabbled with his lately flowing blood;
Seized his hand wistfully, but did not press,
And shrunk as fearful of his own caress;
Enquired into his state: and when he heard
The wound was slighter than he deemed or feared,
A moment's brightness passed along his brow,
As much as such a moment would allow.
"Yes," he exclaimed, "we are taken in the toil,
But not a coward or a common spoil;
Dearly they have bought us—dearly still may buy,—
And I must fall; but have you strength to fly?
'Twould be some comfort still, could you survive;
Our dwindled band is now too few to strive.
Oh! for a sole canoe! though but a shell,
To bear you hence to where a hope may dwell!
For me, my lot is what I sought; to be,
In life or death, the fearless and the free."

VII.

Even as he spoke, around the promontory,
Which nodded o'er the billows high and hoary,

A dark speck dotted Ocean: on it flew
Like to the shadow of a roused sea-mew;
Onward it came—and, lo! a second followed—
Now seen—now hid—where Ocean's vale was hollowed;
And near, and nearer, till the dusky crew
Presented well-known aspects to the view,
Till on the surf their skimming paddles play,
Buoyant as wings, and flitting through the spray;—
Now perching on the wave's high curl, and now
Dashed downward in the thundering foam below,
Which flings it broad and boiling sheet on sheet,
And slings its high flakes, shivered into sleet:
But floating still through surf and swell, drew nigh
The barks, like small birds through a lowering sky.
Their art seemed nature—such the skill to sweep
The wave of these born playmates of the deep.

VIII.

And who the first that, springing on the strand,
Leaped like a Nereid from her shell to land,
With dark but brilliant skin, and dewy eye
Shining with love, and hope, and constancy?
Neuha—the fond, the faithful, the adored—
Her heart on Torquil's like a torrent poured;
And smiled, and wept, and near, and nearer clasped,
As if to be assured 'twas him she grasped;
Shuddered to see his yet warm wound, and then,
To find it trivial, smiled and wept again.
She was a warrior's daughter, and could bear
Such sights, and feel, and mourn, but not despair.
Her lover lived,—nor foes nor fears could blight
That full-blown moment in its all delight:
Joy trickled in her tears, joy filled the sob
That rocked her heart till almost heard to throb;
And Paradise was breathing in the sigh
Of Nature's child in Nature's ecstasy.

IX.

The sterner spirits who beheld that meeting
Were not unmoved; who are, when hearts are greeting?
Even Christian gazed upon the maid and boy
With tearless eye, but yet a gloomy joy
Mixed with those bitter thoughts the soul arrays
In hopeless visions of our better days,
When all's gone—to the rainbow's latest ray.
"And but for me!" he said, and turned away;
Then gazed upon the pair, as in his den

A lion looks upon his cubs again;
And then relapsed into his sullen guise,
As heedless of his further destinies.

X.

But brief their time for good or evil thought;
The billows round the promontory brought
The plash of hostile oars.—Alas! who made
That sound a dread? All around them seemed arrayed
Against them, save the bride of Toobonai:
She, as she caught the first glimpse o'er the bay
Of the armed boats, which hurried to complete
The remnant's ruin with their flying feet,
Beckoned the natives round her to their prows,
Embarked their guests and launched their light canoes;
In one placed Christian and his comrades twain—
But she and Torquil must not part again.
She fixed him in her own.—Away! away!
They cleared the breakers, dart along the bay,
And towards a group of islets, such as bear
The sea-bird's nest and seal's surf-hollowed lair,
They skim the blue tops of the billows; fast
They flew, and fast their fierce pursuers chased.
They gain upon them—now they lose again,—
Again make way and menace o'er the main;
And now the two canoes in chase divide,
And follow different courses o'er the tide,
To baffle the pursuit.—Away! away!
As Life is on each paddle's flight to-day,
And more than Life or lives to Neuha: Love
Freights the frail bark and urges to the cove;
And now the refuge and the foe are nigh—
Yet, yet a moment! Fly, thou light ark, fly!

CANTO THE FOURTH.

I.

White as a white sail on a dusky sea,
When half the horizon's clouded and half free,
Fluttering between the dun wave and the sky,
Is Hope's last gleam in Man's extremity.
Her anchor parts; but still her snowy sail
Attracts our eye amidst the rudest gale:
Though every wave she climbs divides us more,
The heart still follows from the loneliest shore.

II.

Not distant from the isle of Toobonai,
A black rock rears its bosom o'er the spray,
The haunt of birds, a desert to mankind,
Where the rough seal reposes from the wind,
And sleeps unwieldy in his cavern dun,
Or gambols with huge frolic in the sun:
There shrilly to the passing oar is heard
The startled echo of the Ocean bird,
Who rears on its bare breast her callow brood,
The feathered fishers of the solitude.
A narrow segment of the yellow sand
On one side forms the outline of a strand;
Here the young turtle, crawling from his shell,
Steals to the deep wherein his parents dwell;
Chipped by the beam, a nursling of the day,
But hatched for ocean by the fostering ray;
The rest was one bleak precipice, as e'er
Gave mariners a shelter and despair;
A spot to make the saved regret the deck
Which late went down, and envy the lost wreck.
Such was the stern asylum Neuha chose
To shield her lover from his following foes;
But all its secret was not told; she knew
In this a treasure hidden from the view.

III.

Ere the canoes divided, near the spot,
The men that manned what held her Torquil's lot,
By her command removed, to strengthen more
The skiff which wafted Christian from the shore.
This he would have opposed; but with a smile
She pointed calmly to the craggy isle,
And bade him "speed and prosper." She would take
The rest upon herself for Torquil's sake.
They parted with this added aid; afar,
The Proa darted like a shooting star,
And gained on the pursuers, who now steered
Right on the rock which she and Torquil neared.
They pulled; her arm, though delicate, was free
And firm as ever grappled with the sea,
And yielded scarce to Torquil's manlier strength.
The prow now almost lay within its length
Of the crag's steep inexorable face,
With nought but soundless waters for its base;
Within a hundred boats' length was the foe,

And now what refuge but their frail canoe?
This Torquil asked with half upbraiding eye,
Which said—"Has Neuha brought me here to die?
Is this a place of safety, or a grave,
And yon huge rock the tombstone of the wave?"

IV.

They rested on their paddles, and uprose
Neuha, and pointing to the approaching foes,
Cried, "Torquil, follow me, and fearless follow!"
Then plunged at once into the Ocean's hollow.
There was no time to pause—the foes were near—
Chains in his eye, and menace in his ear;
With vigour they pulled on, and as they came,
Hailed him to yield, and by his forfeit name.
Headlong he leapt—to him the swimmer's skill
Was native, and now all his hope from ill:
But how, or where? He dived, and rose no more;
The boat's crew looked amazed o'er sea and shore.
There was no landing on that precipice,
Steep, harsh, and slippery as a berg of ice.
They watched awhile to see him float again,
But not a trace rebubbled from the main:
The wave rolled on, no ripple on its face,
Since their first plunge recalled a single trace;
The little whirl which eddied, and slight foam,
That whitened o'er what seemed their latest home,
White as a sepulchre above the pair
Who left no marble (mournful as an heir)
The quiet Proa wavering o'er the tide
Was all that told of Torquil and his bride;
And but for this alone the whole might seem
The vanished phantom of a seaman's dream.
They paused and searched in vain, then pulled away;
Even Superstition now forbade their stay.
Some said he had not plunged into the wave,
But vanished like a corpse-light from a grave;
Others, that something supernatural
Glared in his figure, more than mortal tall;
While all agreed that in his cheek and eye
There was a dead hue of Eternity.
Still as their oars receded from the crag,
Round every weed a moment would they lag,
Expectant of some token of their prey;
But no—he had melted from them like the spray.

V.

And where was he the Pilgrim of the Deep,
Following the Nereid? Had they ceased to weep
For ever? or, received in coral caves,
Wrung life and pity from the softening waves?
Did they with Ocean's hidden sovereigns dwell,
And sound with Mermen the fantastic shell?
Did Neuha with the mermaids comb her hair
Flowing o'er ocean as it streamed in air?
Or had they perished, and in silence slept
Beneath the gulf wherein they boldly leapt?

VI.

Young Neuha plunged into the deep, and he
Followed: her track beneath her native sea
Was as a native's of the element,
So smoothly—bravely—brilliantly she went,
Leaving a streak of light behind her heel,
Which struck and flashed like an amphibious steel,
Closely, and scarcely less expert to trace
The depths where divers hold the pearl in chase,
Torquil, the nursling of the northern seas,
Pursued her liquid steps with heart and ease.
Deep—deeper for an instant Neuha led
The way—then upward soared—and as she spread
Her arms, and flung the foam from off her locks,
Laughed, and the sound was answered by the rocks.
They had gained a central realm of earth again,
But looked for tree, and field, and sky, in vain.
Around she pointed to a spacious cave,
Whose only portal was the keyless wave,
(A hollow archway by the sun unseen,
Save through the billows' glassy veil of green,
In some transparent ocean holiday,
When all the finny people are at play,)
Wiped with her hair the brine from Torquil's eyes,
And clapped her hands with joy at his surprise;
Led him to where the rock appeared to jut,
And form a something like a Triton's hut;
For all was darkness for a space, till day,
Through clefts above let in a sobered ray;
As in some old cathedral's glimmering aisle
The dusty monuments from light recoil,
Thus sadly in their refuge submarine
The vault drew half her shadow from the scene.

VII.

Forth from her bosom the young savage drew
A pine torch, strongly girded with gnatoo;
A plantain-leaf o'er all, the more to keep
Its latent sparkle from the sapping deep.
This mantle kept it dry; then from a nook
Of the same plantain-leaf a flint she took,
A few shrunk withered twigs, and from the blade
Of Torquil's knife struck fire, and thus arrayed
The grot with torchlight. Wide it was and high,
And showed a self-born Gothic canopy;
The arch upreared by Nature's architect,
The architrave some Earthquake might erect;
The buttress from some mountain's bosom hurled,
When the Poles crashed, and water was the world;
Or hardened from some earth-absorbing fire,
While yet the globe reeked from its funeral pyre;
The fretted pinnacle, the aisle, the nave,
Were there, all scooped by Darkness from her cave.
There, with a little tinge of phantasy,
Fantastic faces moped and mowed on high,
And then a mitre or a shrine would fix
The eye upon its seeming crucifix.
Thus Nature played with the stalactites,
And built herself a Chapel of the Seas.

VIII.

And Neuha took her Torquil by the hand,
And waved along the vault her kindled brand,
And led him into each recess, and showed
The secret places of their new abode.
Nor these alone, for all had been prepared
Before, to soothe the lover's lot she shared:
The mat for rest; for dress the fresh gnatoo,
And sandal oil to fence against the dew;
For food the cocoa-nut, the yam, the bread
Born of the fruit; for board the plantain spread
With its broad leaf, or turtle-shell which bore
A banquet in the flesh it covered o'er;
The gourd with water recent from the rill,
The ripe banana from the mellow hill;
A pine-torch pile to keep undying light,
And she herself, as beautiful as night,
To fling her shadowy spirit o'er the scene,
And make their subterranean world serene.
She had foreseen, since first the stranger's sail
Drew to their isle, that force or flight might fail,
And formed a refuge of the rocky den
For Torquil's safety from his countrymen.

Each dawn had wafted there her light canoe,
Laden with all the golden fruits that grew;
Each eve had seen her gliding through the hour
With all could cheer or deck their sparry bower;
And now she spread her little store with smiles,
The happiest daughter of the loving isles.

IX.

She, as he gazed with grateful wonder, pressed
Her sheltered love to her impassioned breast;
And suited to her soft caresses, told
An olden tale of Love,—for Love is old,
Old as eternity, but not outworn
With each new being born or to be born:
How a young Chief, a thousand moons ago,
Diving for turtle in the depths below,
Had risen, in tracking fast his ocean prey,
Into the cave which round and o'er them lay;
How, in some desperate feud of after-time,
He sheltered there a daughter of the clime,
A foe beloved, and offspring of a foe,
Saved by his tribe but for a captive's woe;
How, when the storm of war was stilled, he led
His island clan to where the waters spread
Their deep-green shadow o'er the rocky door,
Then dived—it seemed as if to rise no more:
His wondering mates, amazed within their bark,
Or deemed him mad, or prey to the blue shark;
Rowed round in sorrow the sea-girded rock,
Then paused upon their paddles from the shock;
When, fresh and springing from the deep, they saw
A Goddess rise—so deemed they in their awe;
And their companion, glorious by her side,
Proud and exulting in his Mermaid bride;
And how, when undeceived, the pair they bore
With sounding conchs and joyous shouts to shore;
How they had gladly lived and calmly died,—
And why not also Torquil and his bride?
Not mine to tell the rapturous caress
Which followed wildly in that wild recess
This tale; enough that all within that cave
Was love, though buried strong as in the grave,
Where Abelard, through twenty years of death,
When Eloïsa's form was lowered beneath
Their nuptial vault, his arms outstretched, and pressed
The kindling ashes to his kindled breast.
The waves without sang round their couch, their roar
As much unheeded as if life were o'er;
Within, their hearts made all their harmony,

Love's broken murmur and more broken sigh.

X.

And they, the cause and sharers of the shock
Which left them exiles of the hollow rock,
Where were they? O'er the sea for life they plied,
To seek from Heaven the shelter men denied.
Another course had been their choice—but where?
The wave which bore them still their foes would bear,
Who, disappointed of their former chase,
In search of Christian now renewed their race.
Eager with anger, their strong arms made way,
Like vultures baffled of their previous prey.
They gained upon them, all whose safety lay
In some bleak crag or deeply-hidden bay:
No further chance or choice remained; and right
For the first further rock which met their sight
They steered, to take their latest view of land,
And yield as victims, or die sword in hand;
Dismissed the natives and their shallop, who
Would still have battled for that scanty crew;
But Christian bade them seek their shore again,
Nor add a sacrifice which were in vain;
For what were simple bow and savage spear
Against the arms which must be wielded here?

XI.

They landed on a wild but narrow scene,
Where few but Nature's footsteps yet had been;
Prepared their arms, and with that gloomy eye,
Stern and sustained, of man's extremity,
When Hope is gone, nor Glory's self remains
To cheer resistance against death or chains.—
They stood, the three, as the three hundred stood
Who dyed Thermopylæ with holy blood.
But, ah! how different! 'tis the cause makes all,
Degrades or hallows courage in its fall.
O'er them no fame, eternal and intense,
Blazed through the clouds of Death and beckoned hence;
No grateful country, smiling through her tears,
Begun the praises of a thousand years;
No nation's eyes would on their tomb be bent,
No heroes envy them their monument;
However boldly their warm blood was spilt,
Their Life was shame, their Epitaph was guilt.
And this they knew and felt, at least the one,

The leader of the band he had undone;
Who, born perchance for better things, had set
His life upon a cast which lingered yet:
But now the die was to be thrown, and all
The chances were in favour of his fall:
And such a fall! But still he faced the shock,
Obdurate as a portion of the rock
Whereon he stood, and fixed his levelled gun,
Dark as a sullen cloud before the sun.

XII.

The boat drew nigh, well armed, and firm the crew
To act whatever Duty bade them do;
Careless of danger, as the onward wind
Is of the leaves it strews, nor looks behind.
And, yet, perhaps, they rather wished to go
Against a nation's than a native foe,
And felt that this poor victim of self-will,
Briton no more, had once been Britain's still.
They hailed him to surrender—no reply;
Their arms were poised, and glittered in the sky.
They hailed again—no answer; yet once more
They offered quarter louder than before.
The echoes only, from the rock's rebound,
Took their last farewell of the dying sound.
Then flashed the flint, and blazed the volleying flame,
And the smoke rose between them and their aim,
While the rock rattled with the bullets' knell,
Which pealed in vain, and flattened as they fell;
Then flew the only answer to be given
By those who had lost all hope in earth or heaven.
After the first fierce peal as they pulled nigher,
They heard the voice of Christian shout, "Now, fire!"
And ere the word upon the echo died,
Two fell; the rest assailed the rock's rough side,
And, furious at the madness of their foes,
Disdained all further efforts, save to close.
But steep the crag, and all without a path,
Each step opposed a bastion to their wrath,
While, placed 'midst clefts the least accessible,
Which Christian's eye was trained to mark full well,
The three maintained a strife which must not yield,
In spots where eagles might have chosen to build.
Their every shot told; while the assailant fell,
Dashed on the shingles like the limpet shell;
But still enough survived, and mounted still,
Scattering their numbers here and there, until
Surrounded and commanded, though not nigh
Enough for seizure, near enough to die,

The desperate trio held aloof their fate
But by a thread, like sharks who have gorged the bait;
Yet to the very last they battled well,
And not a groan informed their foes who fell.
Christian died last—twice wounded; and once more
Mercy was offered when they saw his gore;
Too late for life, but not too late to die,
With, though a hostile hand, to close his eye.
A limb was broken, and he drooped along
The crag, as doth a falcon reft of young.
The sound revived him, or appeared to wake
Some passion which a weakly gesture spake:
He beckoned to the foremost, who drew nigh,
But, as they neared, he reared his weapon high—
His last ball had been aimed, but from his breast
He tore the topmost button from his vest,
Down the tube dashed It—levelled—fired, and smiled
As his foe fell; then, like a serpent, coiled
His wounded, weary form, to where the steep
Looked desperate as himself along the deep;
Cast one glance back, and clenched his hand, and shook
His last rage 'gainst the earth which he forsook;
Then plunged: the rock below received like glass
His body crushed into one gory mass,
With scarce a shred to tell of human form,
Or fragment for the sea-bird or the worm;
A fair-haired scalp, besmeared with blood and weeds,
Yet reeked, the remnant of himself and deeds;
Some splinters of his weapons (to the last,
As long as hand could hold, he held them fast)
Yet glittered, but at distance—hurled away
To rust beneath the dew and dashing spray.
The rest was nothing—save a life mis-spent,
And soul—but who shall answer where it went?
'Tis ours to bear, not judge the dead; and they
Who doom to Hell, themselves are on the way,
Unless these bullies of eternal pains
Are pardoned their bad hearts for their worse brains.

XIII.

The deed was over! All were gone or ta'en,
The fugitive, the captive, or the slain.
Chained on the deck, where once, a gallant crew,
They stood with honour, were the wretched few
Survivors of the skirmish on the isle;
But the last rock left no surviving spoil.
Cold lay they where they fell, and weltering,
While o'er them flapped the sea-birds' dewy wing,
Now wheeling nearer from the neighbouring surge,

And screaming high their harsh and hungry dirge:
But calm and careless heaved the wave below,
Eternal with unsympathetic flow;
Far o'er its face the Dolphins sported on,
And sprung the flying fish against the sun,
Till its dried wing relapsed from its brief height,
To gather moisture for another flight.

XIV.

'Twas morn; and Neuha, who by dawn of day
Swam smoothly forth to catch the rising ray,
And watch if aught approached the amphibious lair
Where lay her lover, saw a sail in air:
It flapped, it filled, and to the growing gale
Bent its broad arch: her breath began to fail
With fluttering fear, her heart beat thick and high,
While yet a doubt sprung where its course might lie.
But no! it came not; fast and far away
The shadow lessened as it cleared the bay.
She gazed, and flung the sea-foam from her eyes,
To watch as for a rainbow in the skies.
On the horizon verged the distant deck,
Diminished, dwindled to a very speck—
Then vanished. All was Ocean, all was Joy!
Down plunged she through the cave to rouse her boy;
Told all she had seen, and all she hoped, and all
That happy love could augur or recall;
Sprung forth again, with Torquil following free
His bounding Nereid over the broad sea;
Swam round the rock, to where a shallow cleft
Hid the canoe that Neuha there had left
Drifting along the tide, without an oar,
That eve the strangers chased them from the shore;
But when these vanished, she pursued her prow,
Regained, and urged to where they found it now:
Nor ever did more love and joy embark,
Than now were wafted in that slender ark.

XV.

Again their own shore rises on the view,
No more polluted with a hostile hue;
No sullen ship lay bristling o'er the foam,
A floating dungeon:—all was Hope and Home!
A thousand Proas darted o'er the bay,
With sounding shells, and heralded their way;
The chiefs came down, around the people poured,
And welcomed Torquil as a son restored;

The women thronged, embracing and embraced
By Neuha, asking where they had been chased,
And how escaped? The tale was told; and then
One acclamation rent the sky again;
And from that hour a new tradition gave
Their sanctuary the name of "Neuha's Cave."
A hundred fires, far flickering from the height,
Blazed o'er the general revel of the night,
The feast in honour of the guest, returned
To Peace and Pleasure, perilously earned;
A night succeeded by such happy days
As only the yet infant world displays.

Lord Byron – A Short Biography

Byron, one of England's greatest poets, endured a quite difficult background. His father, Captain John "Mad Jack" Byron had married his second wife, the former Catherine Gordon, a descendant of Cardinal Beaton and heiress of the Gight estate in Aberdeenshire, Scotland for the same reason that he married his first: her money. Byron's mother-to-be had to sell her land and title to pay her new husband's debts and within two years the large estate of £23,500, had been squandered, leaving her with an annual income in trust of £150. In a move to avoid his creditors, Catherine accompanied her husband to France in 1786, but returned to England at the end of 1787 in order to give birth to her son on English soil.

George Gordon Byron was born on January 22nd 1788, in lodgings, at Holles Street in London although there is a conflicting account of him having been born in Dover.

He was christened, at St Marylebone Parish Church, George Gordon Byron, after his maternal grandfather, George Gordon of Gight, a descendant of James I of Scotland, who, in 1779, had committed suicide.

In 1790 Catherine moved back to Aberdeenshire and it was here that Byron spent his childhood. His father joined them in their lodgings in Queen Street, but the couple quickly separated. Catherine was prone to mood swings and melancholy. Her husband continued to borrow money from her and she fell deeper into debt. It was one of these "loans" that allowed him to travel to Valenciennes, France, where he died in 1791.

When Byron's great-uncle, the "wicked" Lord Byron, died on 21 May 1798, the 10-year-old boy became the 6th Baron Byron of Rochdale and inherited the ancestral home, Newstead Abbey, in Nottinghamshire. However the Abbey was in a state of disrepair and it was leased to Lord Grey de Ruthyn, and others for several years.

Catherine's parenting swung between either spoiling or indulging her son to stubbornly refusing every plea. Her drinking disgusted him, and he mocked her short and corpulent frame. She did retaliate and, in a fit of temper, once called him as "a lame brat", on account of his club-foot, an issue on which we was very sensitive. He referred to himself as "le diable boiteux" ("the limping devil").

Byron early education was taken at Aberdeen Grammar School, and in August 1799 he entered the school of Dr. William Glennie, in Dulwich. He was encouraged to exercise in moderation but could not restrain himself from "violent" bouts in an attempt to overcompensate for his deformed foot. His mother interfered, often withdrawing him from school, and resulting in him lacking discipline and neglecting his classical studies.

In 1801 he was sent to Harrow, where he remained until July 1805. Byron was an excellent orator but undistinguished student and an unskilled cricketer but strangely he did represent the school in the very first Eton v Harrow cricket match at Lord's in 1805.

Byron, always prone to over-indulge, fell in love with Mary Chaworth, whom he met while at school, and thence refused to return to Harrow in September 1803. His mother wrote, "He has no indisposition that I know of but love, desperate love, the worst of all maladies in my opinion. In short, the boy is distractedly in love with Miss Chaworth."

He did finally return in January 1804, and described his friends there; "My school friendships were with me passions for I was always violent." His nostalgic poems about his Harrow friendships, in his book Childish Recollections, published in 1806, talk of a "consciousness of sexual differences that may in the end make England untenable to him".

The following autumn he attended Trinity College, Cambridge, where he met and formed a close bond with John Edleston. On his "protégé" Byron wrote, "He has been my almost constant associate since October, 1805, when I entered Trinity College. His voice first attracted my attention, his countenance fixed it, and his manners attached me to him forever." In his memory Byron composed Thyrza, a series of elegies. In later years Byron described the affair as "a violent, though pure love and passion". The public were beginning to view homosexuality with increasing distaste and the law now specified such sanctions as public hanging against convicted or even suspected offenders. Though equally Byron may just be using 'pure' out of respect for Edleston's innocence, in contrast to the more sexually overt relations experienced at Harrow School. Byron is now thought of as bi-sexual though more fulfilled, on all levels, by women.

While not at school or college, Byron lived with his mother in Southwell, Nottinghamshire. While there, he cultivated friendships with Elizabeth Pigot and her brother, John, with whom he staged two plays for the entertainment of the local community. During this time, with the help of Elizabeth, who copied his rough drafts, he wrote his first volumes of poetry, Fugitive Pieces, which included poems written when Byron was only 14. However, it was promptly recalled and burned on the advice of his friend, the Reverend J. T. Becher, on account of its more amorous verses, particularly the poem To Mary.

Hours of Idleness, which collected many of the previous poems, along with recent compositions, was the culminating book. The savage, anonymous criticism this received in the Edinburgh Review prompted his first major satire, English Bards and Scotch Reviewers in 1809. This was put into the hands of his relative, R. C. Dallas, requesting him to "...get it published without his name". Although published anonymously Byron was generally known to be the author. The work so upset some of his critics they challenged Byron to a duel. Of course, over time, it became a mark of renown to be the target of Byron's pen.

Byron first took his seat in the House of Lords March 13th, 1809. He was a strong advocate of social reform, and one of the few Parliamentary defenders of the Luddites: specifically, he was against a death penalty for Luddite "frame breakers" in Nottinghamshire, who destroyed the textile machines that were putting them out of work. His first speech before the Lords, on February 27th, 1812, sarcastically referenced the "benefits" of automation, which he saw as producing inferior material as well as putting people out of work, and concluded the proposed law was only missing two things to be effective: "Twelve Butchers for a Jury and a Jeffries for a Judge!"

Two months later, Byron made another impassioned speech before the House in support of Catholic emancipation. He expressed opposition to the established religion because it was unfair to people who practiced other faiths.

Out of this period would follow several overtly political poems; Song for the Luddites (1816), The Landlords' Interest, Canto XIV of The Age of Bronze, Wellington: The Best of the Cut-Throats (1819) and The Intellectual Eunuch Castlereagh (1818).

Like his father Byron racked up numerous debts. His mother thought he had "reckless disregard for money" and lived in fear of her son's creditors.

Between 1809 to 1811, Byron went on the Grand Tour, then customary for a young nobleman. The Napoleonic Wars meant most of Europe had to be avoided, and he instead ventured south to the Mediterranean.

There is some correspondence among his circle of Cambridge friends that suggests that another motive was the hope of homosexual experience, and other theories saying that he was worried about a possible dalliance with a married woman, Mary Chaworth, his former love.

But other possibilities exist. Byron had read much about the Ottoman and Persian lands as a child, was attracted to Islam (especially Sufi mysticism), and later wrote, "With these countries, and events connected with them, all my really poetical feelings begin and end."

Byron began his trip in Portugal from where he wrote a letter to his friend Mr. Hodgson in which he describes his mastery of the Portuguese language, consisting mainly of swearing and insults. Byron particularly enjoyed his stay in Sintra that is described in Childe Harold's Pilgrimage as "glorious Eden". From Lisbon he travelled overland to Seville, Jerez de la Frontera, Cádiz, Gibraltar and from there by sea on to Malta and Greece.

While in Athens, Byron met 14-year-old Nicolò Giraud, who became quite close and taught him Italian. Byron sent Giraud to school at a monastery in Malta and in his will, though later taken out, bequeathed him a sizeable sum.

Byron then moved on to Smyrna, and then Constantinople on board HMS Salsette. While HMS Salsette was anchored awaiting Ottoman permission to dock at the city, on May 3rd, 1810 Byron and Lieutenant Ekenhead, of Salsette 's Marines, swam the Hellespont. Byron commemorated this feat in the second canto of Don Juan.

When he sailed back to England in April 1811, he travelled, for a time, aboard the transport ship Hydra, which had on board the last large shipments of Lord Elgin's marbles, a piece of vandalism that Byron had longed railed against. The last leg of his voyage home was from Malta in aboard HMS Volage. He arrived at Sheerness, Kent, on July 14$^{th.}$ He was home after two years away.

On August 2nd, his mother died. "I had but one friend in the world," he exclaimed, "and she is gone."

The following year, 1812, Byron became a sensation with the publication, via his literary agent and family relative R. C. Dallas, of the first two cantos of 'Childe Harold's Pilgrimage'. He rapidly became the most brilliant star in the dazzling world of Regency London, sought after at every society venue, elected to several exclusive clubs, and frequented the most fashionable London drawing-rooms. His own words recall; "I awoke one morning and found myself famous". The Edinburgh Review allowed that Byron had "improved marvellously since his last appearance at our tribunal." He followed up his success with the poem's last two cantos, as well as four equally celebrated "Oriental Tales": The Giaour, The Bride of Abydos, The Corsair and Lara.

His affair with Lady Caroline Lamb (who called him "mad, bad and dangerous to know"), as well as other women and the constant pressure of debt, caused him to seek a suitable marriage i.e. marry wealth. One choice was Annabella Milbanke. But in 1813 he met again, after four years, his half-sister, Augusta Leigh. Rumours of incest constantly surrounded the pair; Augusta, who was married, gave birth on April 15th, 1814 to her third daughter, Elizabeth Medora Leigh, and Byron is suspected to be the father.

To escape from debts and rumours he now sought, in earnest, to marry Annabella, (said to be the likely heiress of a rich uncle). They married on January 2nd, 1815, and their daughter, Ada, was born in December of that year. However Byron's continuing obsession with Augusta and dalliances with others made their marriage a misery.

Annabella thought Byron insane and she left him, taking Ada, in January 1816 and began proceedings for a legal separation. For Byron the scandal of the separation, the continuing rumours about Augusta, and ever-increasing debts were to now force him to leave England.

He passed through Belgium and along the river Rhine and by the summer was settled at the Villa Diodati by Lake Geneva, Switzerland, with his personal physician, the young, brilliant, and handsome John William Polidori. There Byron befriended the poet Percy Bysshe Shelley, and his future wife Mary Godwin. He was also joined by Mary's stepsister, Claire Clairmont, with whom, almost inevitably, he had had an affair with in London.

Kept indoors at the Villa Diodati by the incessant rain during three days in June, the five turned to writing. Mary Shelley produced what would become Frankenstein, or The Modern Prometheus, and Polidori was inspired by a fragmentary story of Byron's, Fragment of a Novel, to produce The Vampyre, the progenitor of the romantic vampire genre.

Byron's story fragment was published as a postscript to Mazeppa; he also now wrote the third canto of Childe Harold.

Byron wintered in Venice, pausing his travels when he fell in love with Marianna Segati, in whose Venice house he was lodging, but who was soon replaced by 22-year-old Margarita Cogni; both women were married. Cogni, who could not read or write, left her husband to move into Byron's Venice house. Their fighting often caused Byron to spend nights in his gondola; when he asked her to leave the house, she threw herself into the Venetian canal.

In a visit to San Lazzaro degli Armeni in Venice, he began to immerse himself in Armenian culture. He learned the Armenian language, and attended many seminars about language and history. He co-authored English Grammar and Armenian in 1817, and Armenian Grammar and English in 1819, where he included quotations from classical and modern Armenian and later, in 1821, participated in the compilation of the English Armenian dictionary, and in the preface he mapped out the relationship of the Armenians with, and the oppression of, the Turkish "pashas" and the Persian satraps, and their struggle for liberation.

In 1817 after a visit to Rome and back in Venice, he wrote the fourth canto of Childe Harold and sold his ancestral home, Newstead Abbey, as well as publishing Manfred; A Dramatic Poem and , Cain; A Mystery.

Byron wrote the first five cantos of his renowned Don Juan between 1818 and 1820. And besides work and adventure there was always love. Women, of course, were always in evidence and the young Countess Teresa Guiccioli found her first love in Byron, who in turn asked her to elope with him. They lived in Ravenna between 1819 and 1821 where he continued Don Juan and also wrote the Ravenna Diary, My Dictionary and Recollections.

It was here that he now received visits from Percy Bysshe Shelley and Thomas Moore.

Of Byron's lifestyle in Ravenna Shelley informs us that; "Lord Byron gets up at two. I get up, quite contrary to my usual custom … at 12. After breakfast we sit talking till six. From six to eight we gallop through the pine forest which divide Ravenna from the sea; we then come home and dine, and sit up gossiping till six in the morning. I don't suppose this will kill me in a week or fortnight, but I shall not try it longer. Lord B.'s establishment consists, besides servants, of ten horses, eight enormous dogs, three monkeys, five cats, an eagle, a crow, and a falcon; and all these, except the horses, walk about the house, which every now and then resounds with their unarbitrated quarrels, as if they were the masters of it… . [P.S.] I find that my enumeration of the animals in this Circean Palace was defective …. I have just met on the grand staircase five peacocks, two guinea hens, and an Egyptian crane. I wonder who all these animals were before they were changed into these shapes."

From 1821 to 1822, he finished Cantos 6–12 of Don Juan at Pisa, and in the same year he joined with Leigh Hunt and Percy Bysshe Shelley in starting a short-lived newspaper, The Liberal, in the first number of which appeared The Vision of Judgment.

For the first time since his arrival in Italy, Byron found himself tempted to give dinner parties; his guests included the Shelleys, Edward Ellerker Williams, Thomas Medwin, John Taaffe and Edward John Trelawney; and "never", as Shelley said, "did he display himself to more advantage than on these occasions; being at once polite and cordial, full of social hilarity and the most perfect good humour; never diverging into ungraceful merriment, and yet keeping up the spirit of liveliness throughout the evening."

Byron's mother-in-law Judith Noel, the Hon. Lady Milbanke, died in 1822. Her will required that he change his surname to "Noel" in order for him to inherit half of her estate. He obtained a Royal Warrant allowing him to "take and use the surname of Noel only". The Royal Warrant also allowed him to "subscribe the said surname of Noel before all titles of honour", and from that point he signed himself "Noel Byron" (the usual signature of a peer being merely the peerage, in this case simply "Byron").

The Shelley's and Williams had rented a house on the coast and had a schooner built. Byron decided that he too should have his own yacht, and engaged Trelawny's friend, Captain Daniel Roberts, to design and construct the boat. It was named the Bolivar.

On July 8th, 1822 Shelley drowned in a boating accident. Byron attended the funeral. Shelley was cremated on the beach at Viareggio where his body had washed up. His ashes were later interred in Rome in the cemetery in Rome where lay already his son William and John Keats.

Byron was living in Genoa when, in 1823, while growing bored, he accepted a call for his help from representatives of the movement for Greek independence from the Ottoman Empire. With the assistance of his banker and Captain Daniel Roberts, Byron chartered the Brig Hercules to take him to Greece. On 16 July, Byron left Genoa arriving at Kefalonia in the Ionian Islands on August 4th.

Byron had spent £4,000 of his own money to refit the Greek fleet and sailed for Missolonghi in western Greece, arriving on December 29th, to join Alexandros Mavrokordatos, a Greek politician with military power. When the famous Danish sculptor Bertel Thorvaldsen heard about Byron's heroics in Greece, he voluntarily re-sculpted his earlier bust of Byron in Greek marble.

Mavrokordatos and Byron planned to attack the Turkish-held fortress of Lepanto, at the mouth of the Gulf of Corinth. Byron employed a fire-master to prepare artillery and took part of the rebel army under his own command, despite his lack of military experience. Before the expedition could sail, on February 15th, 1824, he fell ill, and the usual remedy of bloodletting weakened him further. He made a partial recovery, but in early April he caught a violent cold which further therapeutic bleeding, insisted on by his doctors, aggravated. He developed a violent fever, and died in Missolonghi on April 19th.

Alfred, Lord Tennyson would later recall the shocked reaction in Britain when word was received of Byron's death. The Greeks mourned Lord Byron deeply, and he became a hero. The Greek form of "Byron", continues in popularity as a name in Greece, and a town near Athens is called Vyronas in his honour.

Byron's body was embalmed, but the Greeks wanted their hero to stay with them. Some say his heart was removed to remain in Missolonghi. His body was returned to England (despite his dying wishes that it should not) for burial in Westminster Abbey, but the Abbey refused to accept it on the grounds of "questionable morality".

Huge crowds viewed his body as he lay in state for two days in London before being buried at the Church of St. Mary Magdalene in Hucknall, Nottinghamshire. A marble slab given by the King of Greece is laid directly above Byron's grave.

Byron's friends had raised the sum of £1,000 to commission a statue of the writer by the sculptor Thorvaldsen. However for a decade after the statue was completed, in 1834, most British institutions had refused to accept it, among them the British Museum, St. Paul's Cathedral, Westminster Abbey and the National Gallery, and it remained in storage. Finally Trinity College, Cambridge, placed the statue in its library.

Finally, in 1969, a145 years after Byron's death, a memorial to him was placed in Westminster Abbey. It had been pointedly noted by the New York Times that "People are beginning to ask whether this ignoring of Byron is not a thing of which England should be ashamed ... a bust or a tablet might be put in the Poets' Corner and England be relieved of ingratitude toward one of her really great sons." At last Byron was where he should be.

Lord Byron – A Concise Bibliography

The Major Works
Hours of Idleness (1807)

English Bards and Scotch Reviewers (1809)
Childe Harold's Pilgrimage, Cantos I & II (1812)
The Giaour (1813)
The Bride of Abydos (1813)
The Corsair (1814)
Lara, A Tale (1814)
Hebrew Melodies (1815)
The Siege of Corinth (1816)
Parisina (1816)
The Prisoner of Chillon (1816)
The Dream (1816)
Prometheus (1816)
Darkness (1816)
Manfred (1817)
The Lament of Tasso (1817)
Beppo (1818)
Childe Harold's Pilgrimage (1818)
Don Juan (1819–1824; incomplete on Byron's death in 1824)
Mazeppa (1819)
The Prophecy of Dante (1819)
Marino Faliero (1820)
Sardanapalus (1821)
The Two Foscari (1821)
Cain (1821)
The Vision of Judgment (1821)
Heaven and Earth (1821)
Werner (1822)
The Age of Bronze (1823)
The Island (1823)
The Deformed Transformed (1824)

Index of Titles (This is an abbreviated, not a complete, list of his poems).
A
Address, spoken at the Opening of Drury-Lane Theatre, Saturday, October 10, 1812
The Adieu
Adieu to the Muse (same as "Farewell to the Muse")
Address intended to be recited at the Caledonian Meeting
Adrian's Address to his Soul when Dying
The Age of Bronze (a transcription project)
"All is Vanity, Saith the Preacher"
And Thou Art Dead, as Young and Fair
And Wilt Thou Weep When I am Low?
Another Simple Ballat
Answer to —'s Professions of Affection
Answer to a Beautiful Poem
Answer to Some Elegant Verses Sent by a Friend to the Author, & etc.
Answer to the Foregoing, Addressed to Miss —
Aristomenes
Away, Away, Ye Notes of Woe!

B

Ballad
Beppo, a Venetian Story
The Blues, a Literary Eclogue
Bowles and Campbell
The Bride of Abydos, a Turkish Tale (A transcription project)
Bright Be the Place of Thy Soul! (see "Stanzas for Music")
By the Rivers of Babylon We Sat Down and Wept
"By the Waters of Babylon"

C

Cain, a Mystery (A transcription project)
The Chain I gave (same as "From the Turkish")
The Charity Ball
Childe Harold's Good Night (from Childe Harold's Pilgrimage, Canto I.)
Childe Harold's Pilgrimage
Childish Recollections
Churchill's Grave
The Conquest
The Cornelian
The Corsair: A Tale
The Curse of Minerva

D

Damætas
Darkness
The Death of Calmar and Orla
The Deformed Transformed, a drama (A transcription project)
The Destruction of Sennacherib
The Devil's Drive
Don Juan
A Dream (same as "Darkness")
The Dream
The Duel

E

E Nihilo Nihil; or, An Epigram Bewitched
Egotism. A Letter to J. T. Becher
Elegiac Stanzas on the Death of Sir Peter Parker, Bart.
Elegy
Elegy on Newstead Abbey
Elegy on the Death of Sir Peter Parker (same "Elegiac Stanzas on the Death of Sir Peter Parker, Bart.")
Endorsement to the Deed of Separation, in the April of 1816
English Bards, and Scotch Reviewers, a Satire
Epigram (If for Silver, or for Gold)
Epigram (In Digging up your Bones, Tom Paine)
Epigram (It Seems That the Braziers Propose Soon to Pass)
Epigram (The world is a bundle of hay)
Epigram on an Old Lady Who Had Some Curious Notions Respecting the Soul
Epigrams (Oh, Castlereagh! Thou Art a Patriot Now)

Epilogue
The Episode of Nisus and Euryalus (A Paraphrase from the Æneid, Lib. 9.)
Epistle from Mr. Murray to Dr. Polidori
Epistle to a Friend
Epistle to Augusta
Epistle to Mr. Murray
Epitaph
Epitaph for Joseph Blacket, Late Poet and Shoemaker
Epitaph for William Pitt
Epitaph on a Beloved Friend
Epitaph on a Friend (same as "Epitaph on a Beloved Friend")
Epitaph on John Adams, of Southwell
Epitaph to a Dog
Euthanasia

F
Fame, Wisdom, Love, and Power Were Mine (same as "All is Vanity, saith the Preacher")
Fare Thee Well
Farewell (same as "Farewell! if Ever Fondest Prayer")
Farewell Petition to J. C. H., Esqre.
Farewell to Malta
Farewell to the Muse
Fill the Goblet Again
The First Kiss of Love
A Fragment (Could I Remount the River of My Years)
Fragment (Hills of Annesley, Bleak and Barren)
A Fragment (When, to Their Airy Hall, my Fathers' Voice)
Fragment from the "Monk of Athos"
Fragment of a Translation from the 9th Book of Virgil's Æneid (compare "The Episode of Nisus and Euryalus")
Fragment of an Epistle to Thomas Moore
Fragments of School Exercises: From the "Prometheus Vinctus" of Æschylus
Francesca of Rimini
Francisca
From Anacreon Ode 3. ('Twas Now the Hour When Night Had Driven)
From Job (same as "A Spirit Passed Before Me")
From the French (Ægle, Beauty and Poet, Has Two Little Crimes)
From the French (Must Thou Go, my Glorious Chief)
From the Last Hill That Looks on Thy Once Holy Dome (same as "On the Day of the Destruction of Jerusalem by Titus")
From the Portuguese
From the Turkish (same as "The Chain I Gave")

G
G. G. B. to E. P. (same as "To M. S. G.") (When I Dream That You Love Me, you'll surely Forgive)
The Giaour
The Girl of Cadiz
Granta. A Medley

H
The Harp the Monarch Minstrel Swept

Heaven and Earth, a Mystery (A transcription project)
Hebrew Melodies
Herod's Lament for Mariamne
Hints from Horace (A transcription project)
Hours of Idleness

I

I Speak Not, I Trace Not, I Breathe Not Thy Name (see "Stanzas for Music")
I Saw Thee Weep
I Would I Were a Careless Child
Ich Dien
If Sometimes in the Haunts of Men
If That High World
Imitated from Catullus
Imitation of Tibullus
Impromptu
Impromptu, in Reply to a Friend
In the Valley of Waters (same as "By the Waters of Babylon")
Inscription on the Monument of a Newfoundland Dog
The Island, or Christian and His Comrades
The Irish Avatar
It is the Hour (compare with first stanza of Parisina)

J

Jeptha's Daughter
John Keats
Journal in Cephalonia
Julian [a Fragment]

K

L

La Revanche
Lachin y Gair
L'Amitié est L'Amour sans Ailes
The Lament of Tasso
Lara: A Tale
Last Words on Greece
Lines Addressed by Lord Byron to Mr. Hobhouse on his Election for Westminster
Lines Addressed to a Young Lady
Lines Addressed to the Rev. J. T. Becher
Lines Inscribed Upon a Cup Formed From a Skull
Lines in the Travellers' Book at Orchomenus
Lines on Hearing That Lady Byron Was Ill
Lines on Sir Peter Parker (same as "Elegiac Stanzas on the Death of Sir Peter Parker, Bart.")
Lines to a Lady Weeping (same as "To a Lady Weeping")
Lines to Mr. Hodgson
Lines Written Beneath a Picture
Lines Written Beneath an Elm in the Churchyard of Harrow
Lines Written in an Album, At Malta
Lines Written in "Letters of an Italian Nun and an English Gentleman

Lines Written on a Blank Leaf of The Pleasures of Memory
Lord Byron's Verses on Sam Rogers
Love and Death
Love and Gold
A Love Song. To — (same as "Remind me not, Remind me not")
Love's Last Adieu
Lucietta. A Fragment

M

Maid of Athens, Ere We Part
Manfred, a Dramatic Poem
Marino Faliero, Doge of Venice, an Historical Tragedy (1821) (A transcription project)
Martial, Lib. I. Epig. I.
Mazeppa
Monody on the Death of the Right Hon. R. B. Sheridan
The Morgante Maggiore (A transcription project)
My Boy Hobbie O
My Epitaph
My Soul is Dark

N

Napoleon's Farewell
Napoleon's Snuff-box
The New Vicar of Bray
Newstead Abbey

O

An Occasional Prologue
Ode from the French
Ode on Venice
Ode to a Lady Whose Lover was Killed by a Ball, Which at the Same Time Shivered a Portrait Next His Heart
Ode to Napoleon Buonaparte
An Ode to the Framers of the Frame Bill
Oh! Snatched Away in Beauty's Bloom
Oh! Weep for Those
On a Change of Masters at a Great Public School
On a Cornelian Heart Which Was Broken
On a Distant View of the Village and School of Harrow on the Hill, 1806
On a Royal Visit to the Vaults (Windsor Poetics)
On Being Asked What Was the "Origin of Love"
On Finding a Fan
On Jordan's Banks
On Leaving Newstead Abbey
On Lord Thurlow's Poems
On Moore's Last Operatic Farce, or Farcical Opera
On My Thirty-third Birthday
On My Wedding-Day
On Napoleon's Escape from Elba
On Parting
On Revisiting Harrow

On Sam Rogers (same as "Lord Byron's Verses on Sam Rogers")
On the Birth of John William Rizzo Hoppner
On the Bust of Helen by Canova
On the Day of the Destruction of Jerusalem by Titus
On the Death of — Thyrza (same as "To Thyrza")
On the Death of a Young Lady
On the Death of Mr. Fox
On the Death of the Duke of Dorset
On the Eyes of Miss A— H—
On the Quotation
On the Star of "the Legion of Honour"
On this Day I complete my Thirty-sixth Year
One Struggle More, and I Am Free
Oscar of Alva
Ossian's Address to the Sun in "Carthon"

P
Parenthetical Address
Parisina
Pignus Amoris
The Prayer of Nature
The Prisoner of Chillon
The Prophecy of Dante, a Poem

Q
Quem Deus Vult Perdere Prius Dementat
Queries to Casuists

R
R. C. Dallas
Remember Him, whom Passion's Power
Remember Thee! Remember thee!
Remembrance
Remind Me Not, Remind Me Not
Reply to Some Verses of J. M. B. Pigot, Esq., on the Cruelty of his Mistress

S
Sardanapalus, a Tragedy (A transcription project)
Saul
She Walks in Beauty
The Siege of Corinth
A Sketch From Life
So We'll Go No More A-Roving
Soliloquy of a Bard in the Country
Sonetto di Vittorelli
Song (Breeze of the Night in Gentler Sighs)
Song (Fill the Goblet Again! For I Never Before)
Song (Maid of Athens, Ere We Part) (same as "Maid of Athens, Ere We Part")
Song (Thou Art Not False, But Thou Art fickle) same as "Thou Art Not False, But Thou Art Fickle")
Song (When I Roved a Young Highlander) (same as "When I Roved a Young Highlander")
Song For the Luddites

Song of Saul Before His Last Battle
Song To the Suliotes
Sonnet On Chillon
Sonnet on the Nuptials of the Marquis Antonio Cavalli with the Countess Clelia Rasponi of Ravenna
Sonnet, to Genevra (Thine eyes' Blue Tenderness, Thy Long Fair Hair)
Sonnet, to Genevra (Thy Cheek is Pale with Thought, but Not From Woe). aka "Sonnet, to the Same"
Sonnet to Lake Leman
Sonnet to the Prince Regent
The Spell is Broke, the Charm is Flown!
A Spirit Passed Before Me
Stanzas (And Thou Art Dead, as Young and Fair)
Stanzas (And Wilt Thou Weep When I am Low?) (same as "And Wilt Thou Weep When I Am Low?")
Stanzas (Away, Away, Ye Notes of Woe)
Stanzas (Chill and Mirk is the Nightly Blast) (same as "Stanzas Composed During a Thunderstorm")
Stanzas (Could Love For Ever)
Stanzas (I Would I Were a Careless Child) (same as "I Would I Were a Careless Child")
Stanzas (If Sometimes in the Haunts of Men)
Stanzas (One Struggle More, and I Am Free)
Stanzas (Remember Him, Whom Passion's Power)
Stanzas (Thou Art Not False, but Thou Art Fickle)
Stanzas (Through Cloudless Skies, in Silvery Sheen) (same as "Stanzas Written in Passing the Ambracian Gulf")
Stanzas (When a Man Hath No Freedom to Fight For at Home)
Stanzas Composed During a Thunderstorm
Stanzas For Music (Bright Be the Place of Thy Soul!)
Stanzas For Music (I Speak Not, I Trace Not, I Breathe Not Thy Name)
Stanzas For Music (There Be None of Beauty's Daughters)
Stanzas For Music (There's Not a Joy the World Can Give Like That it Takes Away)
Stanzas For Music (They Say That Hope is Happiness)
Stanzas To — (same as "Stanzas to Augusta": Though the Day of My Destiny's Over)
Stanzas To a Hindoo Air
Stanzas To a Lady, on Leaving England
Stanzas To a Lady, with the Poems of Camoëns
Stanzas To Augusta (When all around grew drear and dark)
Stanzas To Augusta (Though the day of my Destiny's over)
Stanzas To Jessy
Stanzas To the Po
Stanzas To the Same (same as "There was a Time, I need not name")
Stanzas Written in Passing the Ambracian Gulf
Stanzas Written on the Road Between Florence and Pisa
Substitute For an Epitaph
Sun of the Sleepless!
Sympathetic Address to a Young Lady (same as "Lines to a Lady Weeping")

T
The Tear
There Be None of Beauty's Daughters (see "Stanzas for Music")
There Was a Time, I Need Not Name
There's Not a Joy the World Can Give Like That it Takes Away (see "Stanzas for Music")
They say that Hope is Happiness (see "Stanzas for Music")
Thou Art Not False, but Thou Art Fickle

Thou Whose Spell Can Raise the Dead (same as "Saul")

Thoughts Suggested by a College Examination

Thy Days are Done

To — (But Once I Dared to Lift My Eyes)

To — (Oh! Well I Know Your Subtle Sex)

To A— (same as "To M—")

To a Beautiful Quaker

To a Knot of Ungenerous Critics

To a Lady (Oh! Had My Fate Been Join'd with Thine)

To a Lady (This Band, Which Bound Thy yellow Hair)

To a Lady (When Man, Expell'd from Eden's Bowers)

To a Lady Weeping (same as "Lines To a Lady Weeping")

To a Lady who Presented to the Author a Lock of Hair Braided with His Own, and Appointed a Night in December to Meet Him in the Garden

To a Vain Lady

To a Youthful Friend

To an Oak at Newstead

To Anne (Oh, Anne, Your Offences to Me Have Been Grievous)

To Anne (Oh Say Not, Sweet Anne, That the Fates Have Decreed)

To Belshazzar

To Caroline (Oh! When Shall the Grave Hide For Ever My Sorrow?)

To Caroline (Think'st thou I saw thy beauteous eyes)

To Caroline (When I Hear you Express an Affection so Warm)

To Caroline (You Say You Love, and Yet Your Eye)

To D—

To Dives. A Fragment

To E—

To Edward Noel Long, Esq.

To Eliza

To Emma

To E. N. L. Esq. (same as "To Edward Noel Long, Esq.")

To Florence

To George Anson Byron (?)

To George, Earl Delawarr

To Harriet

To Ianthe (The "Origin of Love!"—Ah, why) (same as "On Being Asked What Was the 'Origin of Love'")

To Ianthe (from Canto I of Childe Harold's Pilgrimage) (Not in Those Climes Where I Have Late Been Straying)

To Inez (from Canto I of Childe Harold's Pilgrimage) (Nay, Smile Not at My Sullen Brow)

To Julia (same as "To Lesbia!")

To Lesbia!

To Lord Thurlow

To M—

To Maria — (same as "To Emma")

To Mrs. — (same as "Well! Thou Art Happy")

To Mrs. Musters (same as "Stanzas To a Lady, On Leaving England")

To M. S. G. (When I Dream That You Love Me, You'll Surely Forgive)

To M. S. G. (Whene'er I View Those Lips of Thine)

To Marion

To Mary, on Receiving Her Picture

To Miss E. P. (same as "To Eliza")
To Mr. Murray (For Orford and for Waldegrave)
To Mr. Murray (Strahan, Tonson, Lintot of the Times)
To Mr. Murray (To Hook the Reader, You, John Murray)
To my Son
To Penelope
To Romance
To Samuel Rogers, Esq. (same as "Lines Written On a Blank Leaf of The Pleasures of Memory")
To Sir W. D. (same as "To a Youthful Friend")
To the Author of a Sonnet
To the Countess of Blessington
To the Duke of D— (same as "To the Duke of Dorset")
To the Duke of Dorset
To the Earl of — (same as "To the Earl of Clare")
To the Earl of Clare
To the Honble. Mrs. George Lamb
To the Prince Regent on the Repeal of the Bill of Attainder Against Lord E. Fitzgerald, June, 1819.
(same as "Sonnet to the Prince Regent")
To the Rev. J. T. Becher (same as "Lines: Addressed to the Rev. J. T. Becher")
To the Same (same as "And Wilt Thou Weep When I Am Low?")
To the Sighing Strephon
To Thomas Moore (My Boat is on the Shore)
To Thomas Moore (Oh you, Who in all Names Can Tickle the Town)
To Thomas Moore (What Are You Doing Now)
To Thyrza (Without a Stone to Mark the Spot)
To Thyrza (One Struggle More, and I Am Free) (same as "One Struggle More, and I am Free")
To Time
To Woman
Translation from Anacreon Ode 1. (I Wish to Tune My Quivering Lyre)
Translation from Anacreon Ode 5. (Mingle with the Genial Bowl)
Translation from Catullus: Ad Lesbiam
Translation from Catullus: Lugete Veneres Cupidinesque
Translation from Horace
Translation from the "Medea" of Euripides [Ll. 627–660]
Translation from Vittorelli
Translation of a Romaic Love Song
Translation of the Epitaph on Virgil and Tibullus, by Domitius Marsus
Translation of the Famous Greek War Song
Translation of the Nurse's Dole in the Medea of Euripides
Translation of the Romaic Song
The Two Foscari, a Tragedy (A transcription project)

U

V
Venice. A Fragment
Verses Found in a Summer-house at Hales-Owen
Versicles
A Version of Ossian's Address to the Sun
A very Mournful Ballad on the Siege and Conquest of Alhama
Vision of Belshazzar

The Vision of Judgment (A transcription project)
A Volume of Nonsense

W
The Waltz, an Apostrophic Hymn
Warriors and Chiefs! (same as "Song of Saul Before His Last Battle")
We Sate Down and Wept by the Waters of Babel (same as "By the Rivers of Babylon We Sat Down and Wept")
Well! Thou art Happy
Were My Bosom as False as Thou Deem'st It To Be
Werner, or The Inheritance, a Tragedy (A transcription project)
When a Man Hath No Freedom to Fight For at Home (see "Stanzas")
When Coldness Wraps This Suffering Clay
When I Roved a Young Highlander
When We Two Parted
The Wild Gazelle
Windsor Poetics
A Woman's Hair
Written after Swimming from Sestos to Abydos
Written at Athens (same as "The Spell is Broke, the Charm is Flown!")
Written at the Request of a Lady in her Memorandum Book (same as "Lines Written in an Album, At Malta")
Written in an Album (same as "Lines Written in an Album, At Malta")
Written in Mrs. Spencer S.'s— (same as "Lines Written in an Album, At Malta")